They didn't give Up

OLIVET FACULTY
TELL THEIR STORIES OF
PERSISTENCE

KENT R. OLNEY, EDITOR

Copyright © 2025 by Olivet Nazarene University

978-0-8341-4392-0

All rights reserved. No part of this publication may be reproduced, stored in a retrieval system, or transmitted in any form or by any means—for example, electronic, photocopy, recording—without the prior written permission of the copyright holder. The only exception is brief quotations in printed reviews.

Cover Design: Keylan Salazar Chicaiza
Inside Design: Sharon Page

All Scripture quotations, unless indicated, are taken from THE HOLY BIBLE, NEW INTERNATIONAL VERSION®, NIV®. Copyright © 1973, 1978, 1984, 2011 by Biblica, Inc.® Used by permission. All rights reserved worldwide.

Scripture quotations marked (KJV) are from the King James Version, which is in the public domain.

Scripture quotations marked (NASB) are from the New American Standard Bible®, Copyright © 1960, 1971, 1977, 1995, 2020 by The Lockman Foundation. All rights reserved.

We will not hide them from their descendants;
we will tell the next generation
*the praiseworthy deeds of the L*ORD,
his power, and the wonders he has done.
—Psalm 78:4

As you know, we count as blessed those
who have persevered.
—James 5:11a

*This book is dedicated to
our Olivet Nazarene University students:
past, present, and future*

CONTENTS

Acknowledgments	11
Preface	13
1. When Life Crashes Down *Gregg Chenoweth, President*	17
2. God Is the Persistent One *Jeff Bell, Music*	21
3. Walking Across the Stage *Nancy Bonilla, Modern Languages*	25
4. Crisis in the Yellow Pages *Justin Brown, Mathematics*	30
5. Dreams and Detours *April Clark, Nursing*	34
6. God Puts You Where You Need to Be *Catherine Dillinger, Nursing*	39
7. Impostor Syndrome *Mark Frisius, Theology and Christian Ministry*	44
8. Three Ironies and a Marathon *Lisa Gassin, Psychology*	49
9. My Two Years in the Emergency Department *Tiffany Greer, Nursing*	55
10. Hitting the Wall *Dale Hathaway, STEM*	60

11. Red 54 — 65
    Bruce Heyen, Chemistry

12. Stressed and Sleepless — 69
    Ryan Himes, Biology

13. Airport Tears and Despair — 74
    Andrew Hoag, English

14. The Decision — 79
    Dave Horton, Business

15. Preparation Made the Difference — 84
    Dave Johnson, English

16. From Poverty to Professor — 88
    Marvin Jones, Music

17. Midterm Scare in the Red Room — 93
    Lance Kilpatrick, Education

18. Grief Amidst Milestones — 98
    Elyse Lamszus, English

19. Starting Over, Again — 103
    Stephen Lowe, Academic Affairs

20. Navigating the Unexpected — 108
    Heather McLaughlin, Communication

21. Hurdles in TrackTown — 114
    Kent Olney, College of Arts and Sciences

22. Wooden Hangers — 119
    Beth Patrick-Trippel, Communication

23. Why Me? — 123
    Charles Perabeau, Theology and Christian Ministry

24. Together As One — 128
    Amber Residori, College of Professional Studies

25. Naomi Joy's Footprints *Jeffrey Rice, Computer Science*	133
26. Tears of Persistence *Beth Schurman, English*	139
27. The Creative Process of Persistence *Jon Seals, Art*	144
28. Finishing the Race *Simone Twibell, Theology and Christian Ministry*	150
29. Twins, Triplets, and Tutus *David Van Heemst, Political Science*	155
30. The Best Gift I Never Wanted *Lisa Vander Veer, Student Persistence*	161
31. Sister Mary Rose *Aggie Veld, Biology*	167
32. Love Wins *Laura Widstrom, Theology and Christian Ministry*	171
33. No Background for Success *Neal Woodruff, Music*	175
34. The Olivet Story *John Bowling, President Emeritus*	180
Prayer for Persistence	188

ACKNOWLEDGMENTS

Any book is a group project, and this one is especially so. For starters, thirty-four busy individuals—university professors and administrators—willingly took time to reflect on and then write their stories of persistence. To each of them, I extend my sincere gratitude. This project would have died an early death without you. In addition to contributing to this labor of love, you contribute daily to making Olivet Nazarene University an enjoyable place to work, study, and live.

    Several other individuals deserve special recognition and thanks. Heather Shaner, an Olivet alumna and crackerjack editor, helped us tell our stories in clearer and better ways than we could have done if left on our own. Thank you, Heather, for the hours you committed to clarifying our words, repairing our grammar, and improving our work throughout this process. Keylan Salazar Chicaiza, a member of Olivet's class of 2025 who majored in studio art with a concentration in graphic design, created the book cover. Her artistic eye, capable hands, and winsome spirit made our interactions delightful. Keylan, it has been a joy to work with you. Your work ethic points to a bright future. The team of professionals at The Foundry Publishing offered timely wisdom and valuable direction just when they were most needed. Their collective patience and grace have guided this venture to its successful completion. Bonnie Perry, thank you for entertaining and then framing our project in its early stages; Deanna Bailey, thank you for answering so many questions along the way and keeping us moving forward; and Audra Spiven, thank you for adding the final touches necessary to turn our manuscript into a book. To all of you, and to those who work alongside you at the Foundry, we owe a debt of gratitude. You are an impressive crew.

Finally, this book would never have seen the light of day without the encouragement of Olivet Nazarene University's president, Dr. Gregg Chenoweth; Olivet's vice president for academic affairs, Dr. Steve Lowe; and my fellow Olivet academic deans: Dr. Amber Residori, Dr. Charles Perabeau, Dr. Jonathan Pickering, Dr. Lisa Vander Veer, and Dr. Jay Martinson. Thank you, one and all, for your contributions. Your timely and enthusiastic words of support along the way pushed this project forward and helped us persist until we had a final product.

—Dr. Kent Olney

PREFACE

They Didn't Give Up was written by several Olivet Nazarene University faculty and administrators with their students in mind. Its theme is persistence, defined here as the determination to continue toward completing a goal despite failures, disappointments, obstacles, or setbacks along the way. It means seeing things through to the end rather than getting sidetracked. It entails doing hard things because one understands that the end result will be worth it.

Professors often encourage their students to hang in there when demands increase and life becomes difficult, but less often do they tell their own stories of doing the same. The book you hold in your hands is our attempt to do the latter. We have each paused to reflect on a particular time when life's challenges threatened to overwhelm us and sidetrack us from achieving a goal, in hopes of helping our students realize that the persistence we urge them toward has sustained us too. Truthfully, no one in any generation advances far in life without it.

Persistence has become a dominant theme in higher education in the early twenty-first century. American universities of all stripes are concerned about students not only enrolling in coursework but also continuing until graduation. Strategies to increase university persistence rates abound. Improved advising efforts, increased support staff, monitoring of class size, peer mentors and tutors, and expanded emphasis on the freshman experience are only a few of the attempts to address this need. At Olivet, the concept of persistence was elevated a few years ago to one of our five-year PAVER priorities.[1] Significant attention is given to the topic. This book is a product of that priority: we want to help our students persist through the challenges they are certain to face.

It should be noted that our shared concern about persistence extends far beyond university life and academic rigor. The tenacity needed to keep going when adversity arises is central to success in every stage and area of life. History tells the story of those who persisted. Dr. William Bennett, in his 1993 volume *The Book of Virtues*, includes "perseverance"—a synonym for persistence—as one of ten fundamental virtues required to be a moral and educated people. The virtue is essential to the advancement of civilization. Examples are plentiful: medical researchers persist until they find a cure; inventors persist until they create a product that works; artists persist until their artwork conveys a particular message; engineers persist until a bridge is safe and secure; athletes persist in pursuit of a championship; and political and military leaders persist until victory is won. Very little that we enjoy and take for granted today—electricity, automobiles, magnificent architecture, powerful computers, phones, good music, winning sports teams, and more—came about without persistence from someone. The determination to press forward against all odds is the driving force behind any successful venture. Consequently, although we are concerned about students persisting through college, we also want them to cultivate a lifelong habit of persistence that serves all humanity.

---

1. In 2021 Olivet established five institutional priorities to guide the school over the next five years: Persistence, Affordability, Virtue, Efficiency, and Recruitment. The resulting acronym is PAVER.

Interestingly, the Christian Scriptures speak frequently and favorably about the importance of persistence. Jesus commended persistence when teaching about prayer (see Luke 11:8). Paul linked persistence to doing good and gaining eternal life (see Romans 2:7). Persistence is a spiritual matter that has value far beyond achieving temporary, earthly benefits. Many Old Testament heroes—Job, Joseph, Ruth, David, Jeremiah, Daniel, and Esther, to name a few—are remembered for persisting and succeeding when circumstances looked bleak. "Perseverance," the more commonly used New Testament word, is associated with character (see Romans 5:4); love (see 1 Corinthians 13:7); faith (see Hebrews 11:27); and the endurance of hardship (see Revelation 2:2–3).[2] A careful reading of Scripture makes clear that persistence, or perseverance, is a central attribute of the Christian experience. Simply stated, one's relationship with God—and with anyone else, for that matter—will face tests that require resolve and determination.

Life demands hard things of everyone at one point or another. Sometimes the only choice we have in the matter is *when* we do what is hard. Those who do hard things early in life, such as forgoing immediate pleasures and persisting to get an education, will reap the rewards later when they achieve their desired career. On the other hand, those who make pleasure and play their priority early in life often find hard things waiting for them down the road. This principle holds true outside education as well. For example, those who make financial sacrifices and save early in life are typically able to draw on

---

2. Other key New Testament references to perseverance include the following: 2 Corinthians 12:12; 2 Thessalonians 1:4; 3:5; 1 Timothy 4:16; Hebrews 10:36; 12:1; James 1:3–4, 12; 5:11; 2 Peter 1:6; and Revelation 2:19.

their savings later. Those who intentionally watch their diet, limit junk food, and get proper exercise early in life typically enjoy longer and healthier life. Those who parent selflessly and care for children as young adults enjoy the benefits of grandchildren and a family legacy down the road.

Ultimately, we hope this book will encourage our students to endure when life gets hard. Our prayer is that God will grant you strength and determination to "fight the good fight" (1 Timothy 6:12) when demands, disappointments, and discouragement threaten to derail you. May these stories about your university professors and administrators, who have themselves persisted through many uncertainties and challenges, inspire you to do the same.

A brief word about how the book is organized seems appropriate. *They Didn't Give Up* features stories by both Olivet's current president, Dr. Gregg Chenoweth, and past president, Dr. John Bowling (1991–2021). Their contributions bookend the chapters from faculty members. Readers will be drawn in as Dr. Chenoweth opens by telling the story of persisting through a series of painful personal and family losses. Dr. Bowling concludes the book by sharing the remarkable story of how Olivet exists because its past leaders demonstrated tenacity and determination over the years. Readers will discover that Olivet's history is really the repeated story of persistence during uncertain times. In between these opening and closing chapters, thirty-two faculty contributions are organized alphabetically by the authors' last names.

Some of the stories that follow will bring laughter or a smile; some will result in sadness or tears. Collectively, we hope the stories will inspire our students—and all who read them—to see what is possible when God's grace and human persistence meet.

1
WHEN LIFE CRASHES DOWN*
Gregg Chenoweth

Alongside my parents, the people of the church raised me. Church folk literally carried me around the building as an infant, and I kept attending all my years—every Sunday service, every revival meeting, and every Wednesday youth group session. Dad was on the church board. Mom played the church piano. They co-taught a young adult Sunday school class. Each week, I carried a box of donuts to their room, then raided it for leftovers after the service.

When it came time for college, I chose Olivet, took required courses on the Bible, and made faith in Christ even more my own. I didn't curse or drink booze or doubt God. In my sophomore year, I discovered great alignment for life with a young lady. I wrote Tammy a poem to confess this wasn't "like" but "love" and placed it in her mailbox. She pulled

---

*This chapter is an adaptation of President Chenoweth's chapel message, "Happy in Hardship," delivered August 29, 2024, at Olivet Nazarene University.

me by the wrist under a tree next to the quad, demanding, "Read it to me!" We later married, found a church, tithed our income, and volunteered for various things. We went out for dessert with friends after church softball and basketball games. A house we later owned even had a white picket fence—like a Hallmark movie.

But tragedy struck. Days before my twenty-third birthday, my dad was killed in an airplane crash. We found out while watching CNN. It was the first serious tragedy of my life—the biggest test of my faith. Questions came—*Why did you allow this, God?*—but were short-lived. My family asked me to write the eulogy. I pulled up inner resources to see his death from God's perspective. God didn't kill my dad, but he did permit it. He still loves us; in due time, more hopeful reasons might be revealed.

Under the shadow of Dad's death, a glimmer of light and life glowed: Tammy was pregnant! She literally squealed with excitement. We interpreted the news personally, as a gift from the One called *El Roi*, "the God who sees me." But a couple months later, another tragedy came: miscarriage. Another death devastated and shook our innocent world.

I started to get pretty cranky, spiritually. I wondered to myself, *What is going on here?* Then a few months later, another event rocked us. My part-time job during graduate school was funded by a government grant that was expiring. I lost my income. If you're counting, that's three tough blows within the span of one year.

I must confess that, despite all my earlier advantages in spiritual formation, these events left me agnostic. An atheist believes there is no God; an agnostic is less certain. An agnostic might believe that God exists, but, if he does, he's certainly not personal. He set the world in motion and watches from afar, aloof, unresponsive. This belief stings worse when you know he *could* rescue you but is choosing not to. He sits on the sidelines while all hell breaks loose.

I created a two-column list in my mind. In the left column were all the things I did right for God. On the right was the damage God did to me. I wanted accommodation for my good deeds. I felt that God owed me. So I stopped attending church. I resented how people quoted Scripture to comfort me. I turned off Christian music. Hardship can harden a heart toward God.

This next part is strange and hard to explain. Within about six months, I softened. I felt something beyond words—like kindness and patience from the Holy Spirit, even empathy. Scripture tells us that Jesus is acquainted with our grief and sorrow (see Isaiah 53). It felt like God sat with me in my pain. He who was distant became personal. I began asking myself, *Do I really believe in Jesus? In the Bible? In the modern activity of the Holy Spirit?*

They say the longest distance in the world is twelve inches—from head to heart. I began confronting my doubt with apologetics, a rational defense for the faith. I read a lot of non-biblical texts but also began to encounter Scripture in a fresh way. Faith comes from hearing the Word (see Romans 10:17). That heard Word is *rhema* in Greek, not the written Word *logos*. Faith comes from the living voice of God, an internally experienced truth by the Holy Spirit—just what we need, just when it's needed. John 14:11 landed in my life just when I needed it. Jesus said, "Believe me when I say that I am in the Father and the Father is in me; or at least believe on the evidence of the works themselves." The evidence! God doesn't require blind faith! The longer I looked, the more evidence I found. To this day, I remain satisfied in the truth, reliability, and counsel of the Scriptures for everyday issues.

Are you in the midst of hardship, wondering where God is? Here is a hard teaching. As Samuel Chand writes in his book, *Leadership Pain*, faith has no meaning if pain isn't present. God doesn't shield us from assault or protect us from burden. By permitting us trouble, and setting limits on it, we come into clarity about our own inadequacy and cling to God more closely. God isn't merely a coach through the race of life but "Abba," or "Daddy" (see Hebrews 12). The trouble Daddy permits is nondestructive. My pain didn't destroy me. In fact, I'm supremely confident I wouldn't be in my current position as a Christian university president if God hadn't trained my faith for difficulty. Under the care of the Spirit, I emerged from hardship more committed to my faith, not less.

Ultimately, God is more interested in our wisdom than our wealth, our holiness than our health, our sanctified hearts than our earthly success. Unfortunately, hardship is the most efficient pathway to those eternal virtues. If you're in a spiritual wilderness, perseverance in God is the answer when there are no answers. You can trust God on the journey.

GREGG CHENOWETH, *born and raised in Michigan, is the author of* Everyday Discernment: The Art of Cultivating Spirit-Led Leadership. *He earned a BA from Olivet and a PhD in corporate communication from Wayne State University. After work in journalism and youth ministry and as head of a K–8 Christian school, he entered Christian higher education for a year in Korea, then spent a decade at Olivet in faculty and vice president roles before becoming president of Bethel University from 2013 until 2021. He returned to his alma mater as president in 2021. He is married to Tammy. They have three children and five grandchildren.*

GOD IS THE PERSISTENT ONE
Jeff Bell

God didn't give up, so I can't either. That sounds pretty simple, right? Of course, God is God, and I'm just human. How often I have fallen back on *that* rationalization—*What can I possibly do to make this situation better?* Honestly, although there often are things I can accomplish myself, even against resistance from other people or circumstances, sometimes there really is nothing I can do. Although I don't really view my life as one of struggle—I'm a glass-half-full person—I can remember very clearly times when I was blindsided by disappointment or rejection. While I didn't enjoy those experiences, they are nonetheless part of me now, affecting how and why I do things today. Let me share a few examples.

Music has always been an important part of my life. Through school and church, I was provided many avenues to learn and perform. College gave me the chance to sing at a more professional level, and there were lots of opportunities to audition competitively for performances. At Olivet, where I studied and now teach, there are two big performances featuring student soloists: the annual presentation of Handel's *Messiah* and the commencement concert. I was honored to perform in both events a few times, but there were also times I didn't make the cut. All performers know that much of what happens in an audition is out of their control.

What really stung a couple times was when a judge told me, "We thought you did the best job, but we selected someone else." I'm pretty good at accepting honest criticism from experts, but that really smacked me. If I was the best, why wasn't I selected? And why would someone in authority even *tell* me that? So I did what every mature, reasonable college student would do: I sulked. Then I got mad. Then I realized the short-term outcome wasn't going to change, and I accepted reality. Of course, I didn't know that a couple of the lowest points in my college music life would later have a profound effect on how I deal with my own students who face disappointments, both in music and in other areas of life. When I tell them, "I know how you feel," I really do know how they feel. Those disappointments when I was a student were actually a gift to me to be used for decades of future teaching and interacting with music performers.

Fast-forward to another audition, this time for acceptance into a doctoral program. My paperwork was all in order, but a live performance audition was required. By this time, I had many professional performances on my résumé, and I had just sung a faculty recital that went really well. I was optimistic, even though I had a little fight with seasonal allergies that can do nasty things to a singing voice. The allergies had pretty much cleared up by the time of the audition, and I was sure I could sing through any remaining problems. Instead, I should have done whatever was necessary to reschedule the audition, but I didn't want to postpone entrance to my doctoral work.

Big mistake. The audition didn't go well. The fact that I had done a lot of fine work previously didn't matter to the listeners in that moment. A letter a few days later politely told me I didn't meet their standards of performance. They extended best wishes for the future.

How could I have not followed my own oft-repeated advice to my students about using good judgment on whether to perform when their voices were in bad shape? I was embarrassed both musically and professionally. Then I rationalized that maybe a doctorate wasn't really even necessary. Why go through all this struggle, anyway?

After some consolation and practical words from my dear wife and more than a nudge from a patient heavenly Father, I asked the school for another audition date. They graciously agreed to hear me, and the results were good. In fact, I really admired and respected the members of that committee—some would eventually be my professors in the program—because they had been honest with me about the first audition. They had set and adhered to high standards, which reinforced my commitment to always do the same.

A few years ago, we all went through a bizarre time in history called COVID-19. There's no need for me to recite all of what that entailed. Still, I think we do gain a certain amount of strength and encouragement by sharing our stories, so here's one more. In the fall of 2020, our university resumed on-campus classes, which included lots of new protocols for in-person classroom instruction. Every discipline had to deal with all sorts of things that made interactions with students difficult. In voice classes in particular, we had some unique challenges. How can one teach proper singing technique without seeing a student's mouth? Our state had particularly stringent rules for masks and room occupancies. How does one conduct a sixty-five-voice choir rehearsal when the maximum room occupancy is fifty? We held rehearsals outside in tents, conducted voice lessons with both teachers and students in masks, and even allowed senior recitals to be performed in masks to small audiences spread throughout a large auditorium.

What I began to notice in my students through the hardships we all experienced from life during a pandemic was resilience and persistence. They were adaptive and creative, and they generally maintained good attitudes during that trying time. (My own attitude, on the other hand, needed occasional adjustment.) I saw singers perform a concert spread out across a balcony, singing to the small audience seated below on the lower floor. Our annual Orpheus Choir Variety Show was transformed into individual acts performed in several classrooms around the music building, with audience members moving from room to room in small groups. Our choir even recorded its first music video—not a recording of a concert but a staged video—because we could do it outdoors without masks! Students and faculty decided in many instances that the directive "You won't be able to do that" would be met with the response "We'll do it, but it will look different than we're used to."

Really, isn't that what God tells us many times? You can do it, but it might be in a different way than you expected. I guess when all is said and done, God is the persistent one.

JEFF BELL *was born and raised in southern Michigan. He earned his BS from Olivet and his DA in voice performance and pedagogy from Ball State University. He joined the Olivet faculty in 1997, teaching in the School of Music and directing the Orpheus Choir. Jeff and his wife, Carole, have two daughters and two grandchildren.*

3
WALKING ACROSS THE STAGE
Nancy Bonilla

"You should learn Spanish; it will make you more marketable."

It seemed to be sound advice, so I decided to minor in Spanish. I only needed three classes to complete the minor. And that minor did make me marketable—so marketable that I was hired for my first social work job because of my Spanish minor. There was, however, one small problem: I did not actually have the skills to get beyond a basic conversation in Spanish, let alone perform all the duties required for my position.

This shortcoming became apparent on my first day of work when I had to take a phone call from a Spanish-only speaker. Not only was I unfamiliar with the services my organization offered, but I was not even sure what services this caller needed because I could not read her lips through the phone and could only understand half of what she said! At that point, I realized that learning Spanish was more than a box to check as a strategy to become more marketable; rather, it was the beginning of delightful discoveries on a lifelong journey. While it has not always been easy, it has been one of the most enjoyable journeys I have ever undertaken.

After a year of continuing to learn Spanish on my own, I took a leave of absence from my job and headed to Niños de México, a children's organization I visited in high school. I was convinced that thirty days of immersion would bring my listening skills up to speed. However, thirty days was very different from what God had planned for my life. I was offered the opportunity to teach in the school that Niños was starting that fall. My immediate reaction was to reject the offer because safe, stable, non-risk-taking Nancy does not do things like that. Yet, while I was a student at Olivet, I had committed to following God no matter where he led. So I thought I should probably at least pray about the matter. I remember telling God that I could not do this if it did not feel like home to me. And one day, walking out of the house—approaching day thirty of my month away—San Vicente, Mexico, suddenly felt like home. I knew what I had to do: pack up my things, sell my car, and tell my parents—yes, my sobbing parents—that I was moving to Mexico.

     I spent the next five years at Niños teaching some English, but primarily math and social studies—in Spanish—to high schoolers. I learned all sorts of vocabulary teaching those subjects because "sine" and "cosine" were not terms that naturally came up in my everyday conversations. At the beginning, I traveled around with another *gringa* because she could understand what was being said to us and translate it into English for me, and I would answer in Spanish on our behalf. Listening was easier for her because she was learning Spanish while being in Mexico, whereas I was much stronger speaking and writing the language from my classes. Eventually, I noticed I was not mentally checking out of the hour-long sermons in Spanish and was able to function well in various contexts. Mexico was where I fell in love with teaching, with

Spanish, with Latino culture, and eventually with my husband, Jorge. Nonetheless, after five years, we left Mexico and moved to the United States.

My husband enrolled in grad school, and I needed to work to pay the bills. Again, I was hired because I spoke Spanish, but this time the experience was completely different because I had invested hours of time and effort to learn the language. I confidently and joyfully interacted with Spanish speakers in my financial counseling appointments and served as an interpreter for mental health therapists when the need arose. Yet it was time to make a career change. At the ripe age of thirty, I had finally figured out what career path I wanted to choose for the rest of my life: my goal was to become a Spanish professor. I remember telling my husband that if the opportunity ever opened to teach at Olivet, I would wholeheartedly accept it because Olivet had been such a wonderfully transformative place in my life.

Therefore, I enrolled in the Spanish master's degree program at Illinois State University (ISU), the next step toward becoming a Spanish professor, while my husband completed his graduate work. The graduate degree took me four years to complete. It was not easy; I was no longer a traditional undergraduate student whose "job" was to do well in her studies. I had a full-time job and became a mother for the first time during the program. Sometimes I wished for the simpler life of some of my peers. For example, my son came down with a stomach bug the night before one of my four-hour comprehensive exams, and I was up caring for him rather than sleeping to retain the last few facts I had crammed into my brain. Fortunately, the countless hours of previous studies had paid off, and I successfully finished.

After graduating, I taught at ISU for one year before the call came from Olivet. I had met a current ONU professor in one of my graduate classes, and he recommended me for the job. Some might call it a coincidence, but I knew God had been preparing me precisely for this moment. One little snafu in my plan was that I needed to commit to a doctoral degree in order to work at Olivet. I loved to study, but now I had a new full-time job along with a husband and two small children at home. Would there be enough time and energy in the day to add doctoral studies? I was not sure, but since God had called me to this journey, I trusted he would supply the necessary time and energy when mine ran out. For three years, I taught my students, cared for my children, and completed my studies. I would put my children to bed around 8:00 p.m. and then study for the next four or five hours until I had finished my coursework.

When I started my degree, one of the professors told our class that only 50 percent of us would graduate. Only 50 percent of us would be able to one day call ourselves "Doctor." He took us to the platform where we would graduate and said to picture ourselves walking across the stage. That image stayed with me, and I clung to it, especially during those early-morning study hours. And I did become one of the 50 percent to finish, successfully defending my dissertation on Mexico's Independence Day in 2015. I bought tacos for my Spanish education students to celebrate. Ironically, I never physically crossed the stage my classmates and I had been shown because I wanted to see my students cross their own stage at Olivet's graduation, which was scheduled for the same day.

Learning and teaching Spanish has given me such joy in my life. I know God did not gift me with an exceptional ability to learn another language. Listening is not my strong suit—not even in English! There have been some difficult moments and many times when I have felt like giving up. Yet, if I had given up, I would not have experienced the life-giving moments of human connection that knowing the Spanish language has afforded me. Relaxing around the table and sharing a meal, sweet bread, coffee, or chocolate Abuelita with Spanish speakers has brought me such incredible joy and satisfaction. Seeing what my students can do after four years of language learning has done the same. I am incredibly thankful I get to be part of their journey. And now I regularly encourage them to sit in chapel and picture themselves walking across that stage, not just as college graduates but as *bilingual* college graduates.

A former Spanish student recently contacted me and said, "You were right." She explained that she had given a devotional in one of my classes about persisting through college and encouraging her classmates to "just make it to graduation." Apparently, I told her that difficult moments requiring persistence would not end at graduation. Life often requires persistence. She told me that my comment caught her off guard back then, but now she realizes it was just a taste of reality.

Life is full of stages. So we must persist, grab God's hand, and walk across the next stage.

NANCY BONILLA *was born and raised in Illinois. She earned her BA from Olivet and her EdD in educational psychology from Regent University. Part of the Olivet faculty since 2009, she teaches Spanish and serves as chair of the Department of Modern Languages. Nancy and her husband, Jorge, have four children.*

CRISIS IN THE YELLOW PAGES
Justin Brown

I wish I could remember why I was holding the phone book before I threw it at my former roommate. The phone book—or Yellow Pages, as it was sometimes called—was a thick, heavy book with phone numbers and addresses of businesses organized by category. They were ubiquitous before the internet came along. What was I doing with the phone book at that moment? The superficial answer is that, in preparing for my upcoming move across the country, I had already packed away any device that could connect to the internet, so I was unable to use Google.

    Was I really getting on an airplane the next day to move three thousand miles away? What was I searching the Yellow Pages for that day from my San Diego apartment? Was it the location of a UPS Store so I could send a few boxes of my belongings to Boston ahead of my flight? Maybe I was looking for an answer to the question everyone had been asking me over the last several months: "Why would you want to go to graduate school to study math?"

    My attempt at answering their question with a question of my own never seemed to satisfy anyone: "Why wouldn't everyone want to keep studying mathematics for as long as they could?"

Or maybe I was looking for an answer to the second-most-asked question posed to me over the same time period: "Why would you want to leave San Diego?" (I am still not sure anyone has a good answer to that one.)

Was I looking for the number of a cleaning service? Looking around at my grungy apartment, I realized there was no way I was getting my security deposit back. Maybe I was looking for a life coach or a therapist who could tell me what to do about the ex-girlfriend I knew wasn't right for me but who kept trying to insert herself back into my life.

I doubt it was any of that. I was probably trying to figure out how I was even going to get to the airport the next day. I had been in a car accident the day before, and while no one was injured, my beloved Ford Bronco with primer paint color had been totaled. And although I hadn't been planning to take the car with me to the East Coast anyway (I was supposed to lend the car to my younger brother while I was gone), being without a vehicle for that short timeframe was making this move feel impossible. To top it off, insurance was sure to blame me for the accident, even though the driver of the car in front of me had made an illegal stop in the middle of the highway before I ran into the back of him. Should I be viewing these as terrible omens on the eve of this huge life change I was making? Was I actually going to be able to get on that flight tomorrow? Did I still want to?

I thought I was following God's calling in my life when I made the decision to accept an assistantship at a graduate school on the other side of the continent, where I hardly knew anyone. But doubts were beginning to overwhelm me. Had these doubts been in the back of my mind this entire summer?

Why was I just now recognizing them today? Was I searching the Yellow Pages, or was I having an existential crisis? I had probably been staring at that phone book for quite some time when Tim walked in the door.

Tim had shared the apartment with me but had moved out several months ago. His reasons were completely practical: he found a place to live that was closer to his new job. I knew that but still felt slighted when he left, as if he had weighed our friendship against a more convenient commute, and I had not made a big enough impact on the scales. Earlier that morning I had left him a message about some stuff he had left in the apartment, but amid trying to figure out how to transport my life across the country, I had already forgotten about that. And while wallowing in my self-pity, I did not hear him let himself in the front door with his old key. As he came through the hallway, I was so startled that I threw the phone book in his general direction.

He caught it.

It is amazing how something that felt so impossible while I was all alone became so possible with the support of just one companion. Tim was a true friend that day.

He gave me a ride to the UPS Store, where I sent a few boxes to my future address—*I guess I had better get on that flight tomorrow.*

We found a quick rental vehicle that would get me through the next twenty-four hours—*Maybe I can get on that flight tomorrow.*

We tried our best to clean the apartment with the little time we had left—*We might actually get our security deposit back.*

But most importantly, he gave me friendship on a day when that was what I needed most.

With the benefit of hindsight, it is hard to imagine that I might have given up on my own goals due to a messy apartment and a relatively minor car accident. It might have been technically true that I was moving across the country by myself, but that version of the story does not account for the fact that I had friends, family, and mentors behind me, rooting for my success and absolutely willing to help me out when needed.

The next few days, weeks, months, and years would have plenty of bumps in the road. And we never did get our security deposit back. But I still believe I was following God's calling on my life that day. What if I had let my doubts claim victory and had not gotten on that flight? Would I have completed my graduate degree and found my true vocation as a professor of mathematics? Possibly. Would I have met my future wife and mother of my four children? Doubtful. Of course, we will never know because, as you have probably guessed by now, I got on that flight!

JUSTIN BROWN *has been a professor of mathematics at Olivet since 2009. A native of southern California, he graduated from Point Loma Nazarene University with a BA in mathematics. He completed his PhD at Northeastern University in Boston, focusing on algebraic geometry. While in Boston, he met his wife, Jody, a native of New England. Together, they moved to Illinois, where they are raising their four children.*

DREAMS AND DETOURS
April Clark

When I was three years old, my parents gave me the best Christmas present ever: a doctor's kit with a nurse's cap. From that moment on, I knew what I wanted to be when I grew up. I was going to be a registered nurse.

Fast-forward twenty years or so. I was finally registered for the introductory nursing course at the local community college, ready to fulfill my childhood dream. I was married to a policeman, the love of my life. The future was bright. Life was good.

About that same time, my younger brother was getting ready to graduate from high school. To celebrate, he went out into the hills of southern California with his best friends and some beer. After several hours of drinking and hiking in the mountains, the boys elected my brother to drive back down the mountain because he was the least drunk among them all. It was two weeks before his eighteenth birthday. On the road heading down the mountain, my brother crossed the center line and hit another vehicle head-on. My brother and the other driver were the only survivors. All his friends, and the single passenger in the other vehicle, died. And the accident was without question my brother's fault.

Getting a phone call after 9:00 p.m. is never good news. While my husband was at work, I headed to the hospital with my parents to see my brother, maybe for the last time. Because he had broken the law, the emergency room staff thought it would be wise and less threatening if I saw my brother prior to my parents entering the room. So I was ushered in alone to see him before he was cleaned up. When I got to the bedside, I was unable to recognize my baby brother. The sight was horrifying. His forehead was basically lying on his right cheek. He was convulsing and covered with road rash.

Seeing my brother in that condition was unspeakably hard. I felt sick to my stomach. I felt lightheaded. I thought I was going to pass out. As I sat on a hard plastic chair in the ER waiting for the nurse to bring me a glass of water, I thought, *My dream is over. If this is what nursing is, I can't do it.* I went into the hall and called my husband at work, crying. "I can't be a nurse," I told him. He spoke to me calmly and simply told me to change my major and go into business. I did as he suggested: detour number one.

Fast-forward another ten years. By then I was a mother and had been working as a full-time bookkeeper for several years. However, during that season of life, I kept feeling the call and passion of caring for others heavy on my heart. I prayed and prayed. Then I talked to my husband about going back to school. When he asked what I was going to do, I simply said, "I'm going to be a nurse." Within three years, I finally had my RN license.

I continued my nursing education over the next decade and even started work on my PhD in nursing education. When it came time for our daughter to get ready for college, my husband and I began planning for our retirement. Again, life was good.

Then my husband got injured at work. It all began with a twisted ankle he endured while in a foot pursuit. At the time, it seemed relatively minor with no fracture detected. But months later, and after recurring pain, we discovered he had fractured his ankle after all. To make matters worse, the lack of timely and proper treatment of the fracture had severed the tendons and ligaments in his ankle. The increased damage required surgery. We were hopeful the surgery would correct the harm that had been done. Though the surgery was a success, my husband was a stubborn patient and refused to walk as advised.

One month after the surgery, I awoke and headed off to work like I always did. My husband and daughter were scheduled to take my father-in-law to his oncology appointment later that day. Much to my surprise, however, I received a text from our daughter indicating that my husband of twenty-six years was being taken to the hospital, unresponsive.

I immediately left work and tore off down the freeway. I'm sure I was going at least 110 miles per hour. When I got to the hospital, I followed the nurse into the room where my husband was supposed to be. Instead, I found my daughter and sister waiting there. One look at my sister's face told me all I never wanted to know.

In reaction, I threw my ten-pound purse at her head. I'm very thankful that she ducked!

My husband, the love of my life, was dead of a massive saddle pulmonary embolism—a blood clot blocking the flow of blood to both lungs.

In the aftermath, I was left to deal with insurance companies, bills, the mortuary, the funeral, and the police department. I was numb. My schoolwork for my doctorate was the last thing on my mind. I called my school and withdrew from classes: detour number two.

Five years later, I was on a healing road trip that took me across the country and back. I stopped to visit childhood friends. I went to places I hadn't seen before. I drove through Wyoming and met new friends. While there, I was told of a job opening for a nursing professor in Wyoming. On a whim, I applied for the position and got hired a month later.

My new boss was a big believer in education. When she discovered that I had started but not completed my doctoral degree, she encouraged me to go back and finish. Almost seven years had passed in the interval. I thought maybe it was too long. I prayed, asking God if that was what he wanted for me. Soon, I was accepted back into my original program.

Doctoral studies require coursework appropriate to the specific major. After completing the courses, students take a written test called a comprehensive examination. While the particular details may vary, in my program this meant writing three papers to answer three specific questions. The point was to prove subject mastery and an ability to write before beginning a dissertation.

I completed the coursework, got assigned my three questions, and started on my comps. I was sure I could write. I was also sure I had mastered the necessary concepts. Therefore, I was confident I would finish successfully. I didn't. I failed: detour number three.

When I got the results back indicating I had not passed, I was devastated. I had never failed at anything. All I could think was that I should just quit. I convinced myself I didn't need a PhD to be a nursing professor. I didn't need it for my job. It was just something I had dreamed about and never finished before my husband died.

But that was just the problem: it was something left unfinished. It was an incomplete in my life. So I went back to prayer. I prayed for the answer and for peace. When I thought of quitting, I was agitated. When I thought of sticking it out, redoing the exam, and finishing my degree, I had peace. That eventually led me back to the computer, and I started typing again. I graduated with my doctoral degree eight months later.

We all have dreams. God gives us these dreams to fuel our passions and our gifts, which come from him. But life is full of detours. The detours can become distractions that separate us from our dreams, gifts, and passions. Death is the biggest detour of all. But God conquered even death. That means his Son, Jesus Christ, is alive and able to dwell within us—making it possible for us to overcome and persist in reaching our dreams.

APRIL CLARK *was born in North Carolina and spent her early years in Pennsylvania, Ohio, and California. She earned a BSN from California Baptist University and her PhD in nursing education from Capella University. In 2021 she moved from Wyoming to join the faculty at Olivet, where she is an associate professor of nursing. She shares her home with her mother, a dog, and two cats. She has an adult daughter.*

GOD PUTS YOU WHERE YOU NEED TO BE
Catherine Dillinger

My story is not about someone who dreamed about her future career from childhood, put a plan in place, and achieved that goal soon after graduating. It took me a lot longer to get where I am today. As the youngest of four children, I was the only one of my siblings who was still living at home by the time I got to high school. I worked and went to school, and at some point, I remember sitting down with my dad and having a life talk. My father was a man of few words, but what he did say always made an impact on me.

One night we were talking about my brother Paul. He was born about six years before me and died at nine months. He had Down syndrome and a heart anomaly that, at the time, they could not fix. As part of our conversation, my father told me about Misericordia Home, which was located not far from where we lived on the southwest side of Chicago. Misericordia provides residential services for those with intellectual and developmental disabilities. I volunteered at Misericordia that summer, and that was when I decided to venture into nursing.

My plan was to graduate from high school and then join the Army to pursue a nursing career. My father had quite a story from his own experiences in the Army during World War II, and his story contributed to my desire to join the military. However, sometimes our plans are not God's plans, and that was the case for me.

In my senior year of high school, my dad had a bad stroke. He was in the hospital for two and a half months, and when he came home, it was clear he was never going to return to being the Daddy I knew in the past. The prognosis was that he would live three or four years. Because of the care my mother gave him, he lived twenty-three more years! My mother never had any medical training but had experience taking care of my grandparents while also caring for her two young children and mourning the loss of a third child. She was adamant that my father would never go to a nursing home. Thus began my nursing education. We all helped; we did what we had to do. Because of the care my mother provided to my father—and the example she showed all of us in the process—my children had the opportunity to know their grandfather. For that, I will be eternally thankful to her.

Life immediately changed for me in the aftermath of my father's stroke. There was no longer an Army or nursing career to pursue. Because I was the last one at home, I helped Mom and went to work in downtown Chicago. As some like to say, life happened. I married, had children, then divorced. Nursing school became a dream that faded into the distant past. It was a missed opportunity that I assumed was lost forever.

When I met my current husband, Frank, we were both working at a call center and both going through divorces, so we became good friends. We each declared we would never remarry. God had different plans. On September 11, 2001, the world was rocked with what would come to be known as 9/11. We buried my father the next day. I have often said that 9/11 would have killed him if he had been alive to witness it. He was a true patriot.

As we planned a small wedding and built new relationships within Joliet First Church of the Nazarene, my soon-to-be husband prepared for the inevitability of deploying with the Army Reserves. At the same time, the call center was closing, and I knew I would be one of about nine hundred who would lose their jobs. That was when Frank suggested I go to nursing school because I had lost the chance earlier in life.

I laughed. It was too late, and I was too old. But then I thought, *Should I pass up the opportunity to fulfill a dream?*

That is how my nursing career began. My new husband deployed to Iraq and would be gone for almost sixteen months while I began the trek through nursing school to become a registered nurse. Often, I look back and wonder just how I got through that time. Communication with my husband was spotty, the political-military situation was scary, and nursing school was hard. Yet, through it all, I had an unbelievable church family and the belief that if I placed my life and these uncertainties in God's hands, everything would work out.

The Guinness Book of World Records once declared the bachelor of science in nursing (BSN) degree to be the world's hardest to achieve. I can attest to that. Frank came back from his military service, and our life together continued. Then a few years later, when I was thirty-eight, I went back to school for my BSN. My husband had just earned his MBA at the time, and I clearly remember looking at his master's degree and stating, "I will never be smart enough to earn a master's degree."

Not long after that, a friend of mine suggested we do the master of science in nursing (MSN) program together. That is how I initially came to Olivet. I took all my MSN classes and was blessed to be able to do my precepting hours at ONU. The main reason I wanted to acquire my MSN was so that, as Frank and I planned to make a move to Kentucky in the summer of 2016, it would open more doors for teaching. Looking back now, we laugh, and I always feel like God truly has a sense of humor. He knew my plan, but it was not his plan. At the end of my precepting hours, ONU offered me a full-time assistant professor position. After a lot of prayer and conversation, we knew that Bourbonnais was where we would be for quite a while.

In May 2016, I walked across the stage to receive my MSN. I remember my mother being so proud and telling me, "Daddy would have been so very proud of you." It was one of my biggest blessings to share that special moment with her. That December, my mother passed away.

In August 2022, I completed my PhD in nursing education with my dissertation focusing on a topic I knew all too well: persistence. It was a pivotal moment for me. I often look back on my life and the path I have traveled. Not much went the way I thought it would go. If someone had told me I would go back to school at age thirty-eight and become a nurse, I would have laughed in the person's face. Now, I have a PhD and am the associate dean for ONU's School of Nursing. I took one step at a time, one task at a time, and kept going forward. Was it easy? Of course not. There were more tears along the way than I ever thought possible. But I learned to keep going and celebrated each victory, no matter how small.

I have titled this essay "God Puts You Where You Need to Be." Let me add that he does so just *when* you need to be there. Never would I have imagined the plans God had for me, but he did. He gave me the strength to realize I could continue taking those steps, one at a time, to make my dream—that I thought I had lost at eighteen—come true.

I remind my students of this truth several times a semester because they can get so discouraged. They may fail a class, get sick, and need to repeat a course or even an entire semester, and they feel like it is the end of the world. It isn't. It's just a bump in the road. I try to encourage them to do what they need to do, push forward, and let God take care of the rest. He already has it all planned out. Our part is to keep going, to persist.

CATHERINE DILLINGER *was born and raised in Chicago, Illinois. She earned an AAS/RN from Joliet Junior College, a BSN from Purdue University, and a PhD in nursing education from Capella University. Cathy joined the Olivet School of Nursing faculty in 2016, teaching fundamentals, obstetrics, and introductory courses. She also served as the program director for the School of Nursing before becoming the associate dean of nursing in 2025. Cathy and her husband, Frank, share two children and three grandchildren.*

IMPOSTOR SYNDROME
Mark Frisius

Earning a doctorate can be a long journey filled with ups and downs. It often requires a meshing of personalities between student and director, along with a healthy dose of self-confidence. It's difficult to complete coursework and a dissertation without truly believing you're a competent scholar and without possessing a distinct sense of persistence.

One of the areas I struggled with during my graduate programs was believing I could measure up in the intellectual realm. Experts have a term for it: "impostor syndrome." It is the belief that you don't belong and the fear you'll be discovered. I didn't struggle with it while I was working on my master's degree. I was confident and knew that I was going to be a professor, all while resting in the assurance that I was smart enough and everyone would recognize that.

I assumed that the process of applying for doctoral programs would be a breeze because they would recognize my brilliance and realize how much they needed me. It came as a shock when I received all my rejection letters on the same day. My confidence was shaken, and I worried that my entire future was going up in smoke. That evening, I called one of my mentors from college. Although he did encourage me, he also let me know that one of my former classmates had gotten into a great doctoral program. This was the same classmate who had brushed off classes, rarely turned in quality work, and was the prototypical jock. I couldn't believe he had gotten in and I'd been left out in the cold. At the time, I was certain that my dream of becoming a professor was at an end. I had been discovered as an impostor.

A few months later, I graduated from seminary, and my wife and I took a gap year from school and discovered that God had a different plan for how things would work out. We ended up teaching at a small Bible college in Kyiv, Ukraine. This opportunity gave us time to reset and consider how we might move forward. I ended up submitting additional applications to doctoral programs and waited for the responses. I assumed I would receive additional rejections, and I prepared to spend an additional year in Kyiv. However, my persistence paid off, and I was accepted into a doctoral program following my gap year.

The entire program was a gigantic test of persistence. We lived on the other side of the United States from where our family and friends were (although it was nice to be back in the same country). We had a small, one-bedroom apartment in Washington, DC, which wasn't ideal for two people from small towns. Just driving around DC would be a test of perseverance in and of itself. To top things off, the director of my program was standoffish and didn't seem to think I should be there. In fact, in her comments on one of my papers, she told me I probably wouldn't finish and should consider withdrawing from the program.

That moment is burned in my memory. I was already thinking I didn't belong and was struggling with that same impostor syndrome; here was further confirmation from an outside source. The crisis forced a decision. Was I going to persist toward what I believed I was called to do, or would I give up and do something easier? Looking back, I'm not sure if it was perseverance or stubbornness (perhaps both) that caused me to stay, but I did stay. I finally completed all my coursework. My wife's encouragement played a big role in the achievement.

Then it was time to write a dissertation—or, as my dad referred to it, my "little paper." Writing a dissertation is an involved process that takes a high level of coordination with a dissertation advisor. The first step is to write a formal proposal, which must be approved by the advisor and two readers then vetted by an oversight committee (usually a group of two to three scholars in related disciplines). It was a nerve-wracking process, especially considering that my dissertation advisor was the same program director who had earlier suggested I should drop out. By this point I had at least convinced her I would be able to finish, and I submitted my proposal. Two days prior to defending the proposal before the oversight committee, I was summoned to the office of the committee chair. This was something neither I nor any of my friends had ever heard of and immediately made me think my proposal had already been rejected—welcome back, impostor syndrome.

However, the news was quite different. My dissertation advisor had quietly accepted a different position and was leaving the university at the end of the semester, which was only about three weeks away. The committee had never experienced this sort of situation before and took a lot of time deciding whether I could move forward or would need to start all over with a different advisor. I was eventually told I could still defend my proposal, but, if approved, I would have to write my dissertation on my own until a replacement was hired. Hooray! Yet another chance to persist!

The topic for the dissertation was approved, and I was allowed to move into the phase of writing what would become a nearly five-hundred-page work without the benefit of a supervisor for much of the process. There were several times when I wanted to throw up my hands in frustration and give up, but I kept at it. The pile of books in our tiny apartment grew and grew while I plugged away without any idea of how my work would be received. As I neared the start of chapter five out of seven, two things happened. The university hired a supervisor, and I started looking for a job. Although he had been selected in October, my new supervisor couldn't work with me until he officially started work at the university in August (ten months later), at which point I hoped I would be nearly finished.

Looking for a job also provided multiple opportunities to persist. One of the challenges I faced was finding a Christian university that needed an early church historian—those opportunities are few and far between. As I sent out my applications to the few schools that were hiring, I was met with a wall of silence. Few schools acknowledged they had received my application, and even fewer notified me of their verdict. It wasn't until March that I received my first phone interview with a school in Georgia. It was one of those experiences where I learned a great deal about what I should have done to prepare. In other words, I bombed the interview and welcomed back the impostor syndrome. With that failure under my belt, I figured I wouldn't get a position until the next round of faculty hirings that typically begin in October or November. Thus, I pretty much stopped looking for openings.

In April, however, my wife convinced me to look one more time, and I found an older post for a Nazarene university in Illinois with a position that sounded tailor-made for me. The window for applying had closed two days earlier, but I hurriedly put together my application anyway, submitted it, and received a response that they were about to interview a candidate to whom they expected to offer the position. Well, there it was: a perfect position for me, going to someone else. But three days later, Olivet contacted me for a phone interview because there had been a change regarding the previous candidate. Three months after that, I said farewell to the impostor syndrome, headed for Illinois with my wife, and saw that particular season of persistence come to an end.

MARK FRISIUS, *born in California, grew up just outside Portland, Oregon. He earned his BA from George Fox University and his PhD in church history from The Catholic University of America. He began teaching at Olivet in 2008 and is currently a professor of theology and the director of undergraduate programming in the School of Theology and Christian Ministry. He and his wife, Ellen, have two sons.*

THREE IRONIES AND A MARATHON
Lisa Gassin

The *Merriam-Webster Dictonary* defines irony as "incongruity between the actual result of a sequence of events and the normal or expected result."

I headed off to college as a newly minted seventeen-year-old, younger than almost all my classmates. Despite my age, I had a decent academic record from high school and was optimistic about my university studies. I chose human development as my major, which is like a subarea in psychology called developmental psychology. It is basically the study of change across the human lifespan. I also had four years of high school Spanish under my belt and assumed that continuing language study would be wise. (For those raised in California, it's hard to miss the fact that many people in the United States were Spanish speakers before they were English speakers.)

I don't recall every class I took as I began my college studies, but I can tell you for sure that Introduction to Psychology and whatever Spanish I tested into were among them. At some point that first year, I also took Introduction to Sociology. I remember these classes because I *tanked* them. My Intro to Psych grade was the lowest actual grade I received my freshman year; it may have been the lowest grade of my entire college career. I didn't get real grades in Spanish or Intro to Sociology because, after doing so poorly, I filed to take them as pass/fail so they wouldn't affect my GPA.

I have no idea how to explain my lackluster performance in Intro to Psych. The section I was in was taught by a well-known developmental psychologist, so I should have been in my element. Regarding Spanish, the subjunctive verbs killed my spirit. In Intro to Sociology, we were reading a lot of primary sources, and I think the readings were too abstract for my still-developing brain. At least, that's how I remember those classes. It was a long time ago, and—spoiler alert—since I went on to get a PhD in psychology, I'm now quite familiar with how unreliable our memories are.

That first year and those specific classes were a real wake-up call. I learned that, although it is good to have fun in college, studying and classwork need to be the priority. My "job" at that time was being a student, and that role needed the majority of my attention. By the time I reached the end of my undergraduate career, my grades and other relevant professional experiences were strong enough to get me into graduate programs in educational psychology/human development, first at Purdue University for a master's degree and then at the University of Wisconsin-Madison for my doctorate.

You've probably already caught irony number one: a bad experience in the most fundamental course of my undergraduate studies—Introduction to Psychology—didn't keep me from letting God pick me up and help me succeed in the field. I had to do my part, of course, since he doesn't force himself or his help upon us. The second irony, perhaps less obvious, is that, although I really bombed in that first sociology class, I'm now a professor in a department that houses Olivet's sociology program. I've taken a class in that program and enjoyed it immensely. Perhaps crazier still, I've even published a few academic papers on religious ritual that can probably be more reasonably categorized as sociology than psychology.

The final irony concerns foreign-language studies. I hit a wall with Spanish, which could have turned me off to studying another language for good. But it didn't. I grew up during the second half of the Cold War, when the USA and Russia were bitter enemies. Born to a patriotic father, I think it was my stubbornly rebellious streak that contributed to my falling in love with Russia. (I also became a Los Angeles Dodgers fan for a while as a teenager, which broke his San Francisco Giants-lovin' heart. You see what kind of adolescent I was!) I fell in love with Russian literature, their figure skaters in the Winter Olympics, their tragic revolutionary history—the whole nine yards. I wanted to study Russian but wasn't sure how to make that work. After all, I was about to go to grad school, where I would be eating and breathing psychology, not Russian, for the next seven years of my life.

We can debate whether there is such a thing as a true coincidence. I'm not sure I have a firm opinion on that issue. However, there were some events that were so weird and unexpected, I can only suspect the Lord actively arranged the circumstances. In my PhD program, I spent the first year as a teaching assistant (TA) for my advisor, who taught one section of the undergraduate course in adolescent development. I was required to attend large lectures and host regular office hours to assist students who wanted help. I was slated to serve in the same capacity in my second year, but the two professors who taught different sections of the class decided at the last moment to swap TAs. They asked me to switch to the other professor, which meant that, in addition to attending a large lecture, I would also be leading several required discussion sections for students each week. These discussion sections allowed me to get to know the students much better.

Oddly, a professor from a department across campus was a student in the section of the course for which I was then the TA. He was taking the class to become certified as a high school teacher. The certification was intended to help him as he worked with preservice teachers in his own department at the university. You may have guessed the department in which he worked: indeed, it was the Department of Slavic Languages, and he was a professor of Russian with a special interest in second-language learning. Making his acquaintance was all I needed to get myself into Russian 101 the next semester. This professor turned out to be an amazing mentor, helping me find funds to continue my grad program in psychology for an extra year so that, simultaneously, I could go as far in the undergrad Russian program as possible.

After finishing my PhD, I came straight to Olivet to teach. One might think that landing in a charming cornfield outside Chicago would make my studies in Russian irrelevant. One would be wrong. I had summers to visit my adopted homeland, Russia, and the ONU administration was flexible in allowing me a leave of absence to pursue extended periods of time there. I will be forever grateful to those at ONU who supported me in these endeavors. And, although for various reasons (including a pandemic) I haven't been on Russian soil since 2018, these days I'm easily able to stay connected with my Russian friends via technology. Thanks be to God!

I'm reminded that the Lord has a funny way of redeeming our failures. We see this truth woven throughout Scripture (think snooty younger brother Joseph of the Old Testament and all too brazen Peter of the New). My story is a small continuation of this theme. Whereas early on I choked in my studies of psychology and sociology, for my entire career thereafter, I have been swimming in those waters with some success. Difficulties mastering one grammatical category almost killed my interest in foreign language. Yet an odd coincidence in grad school turned that around and led to me coming close to mastering a language the U.S. Foreign Service Institute considers much more difficult than Spanish. (That may be, but the Russian subjunctive is far easier!) God opened doors, and I walked through them.

These are areas of my life that have worked out. However, readers need not surrender to discouragement if they are feeling beaten down and see no deliverance in sight. Believe me, there are other areas in my life where difficulties have been present for years. I think the lesson I have learned from these three ironies is that, while there will always be troubles (see John 16:33), it's important to understand that life is a marathon. The apostle Paul regularly uses the metaphor of a footrace to describe his life (see, for example, Galatians 2:2; 2 Timothy 4:7). We must work hard to achieve goals. The race *will* have rough patches; we *will* fall. But God *will* pick us up if we let him, and if we stick to the process, we *will* find that his grace is sufficient (see 2 Corinthians 12:9) to get us across the finish line.

LISA GASSIN *was born and raised in northern California. She holds a BS in human development from the University of California-Davis and a PhD in educational psychology/human development from the University of Wisconsin-Madison. Lisa joined the Olivet faculty in 1995 and teaches numerous psychology courses. She also serves as the associate dean of institutional effectiveness. Her extended family lives on the West Coast, so in Illinois she has surrounded herself with four-legged, furry roommates.*

MY TWO YEARS IN THE EMERGENCY DEPARTMENT
Tiffany Greer

I wanted to be a nurse since the age of four. I often played nurse with my older sister, wrapping her leg in a blanket cast or tying a string to a baggie and hanging it as her IV on my canopy bed. I had a nursing kit with candy pills, a hot water bottle, and a plastic stethoscope. My future career was determined.

Fast-forward to my life as a nurse after graduation. The work was really challenging—but very rewarding. I felt I made a difference in the lives of my patients and enjoyed working as a team with my fellow nurses. After completing my master's degree in nursing, I began to teach nursing at the university level while still maintaining my role in the emergency department (ED) on holidays and in the summers. Due to various life circumstances, I left my teaching role to become a part-time clinical nurse educator in the ED, which allowed me to be home with my four-year-old daughter and infant son more while still doing what I loved: nursing and education.

The difficulty began when I started job-sharing. I think of myself as pretty easy to get along with. I like to see the best in people and find solutions to accommodate others' needs.

But this situation was one I could not seem to impact. The person I job-shared with disregarded my knowledge and my ideas and would physically demonstrate her authority over our office and educational space. She would plan events without my input and belittle my contributions. It was defeating both emotionally and professionally. I began to pray for God to help me find a different job. I did not feel I could go back to teaching at that time, and other opportunities within the hospital never seemed to work out. I felt stuck.

I have learned along life's way that being stuck is fertile ground for persistence. Such situations become times when I am forced to take my gaze off what is uncomfortable, defeating, and hard, and look up. What is God teaching me in this moment? How can he still use me? Over the two years that I worked as an educator in the ED, I can point to four different instances where God showed me why I needed to be in that place, at that particular time, for certain people.

The first was a brief interaction with a drug representative. She was there to speak with the nurses, and it was a busy time. We stood there chatting while waiting for everyone to gather. For some reason, she began sharing about her marriage difficulties, and I was able to encourage her and point her to consider counseling to help her and her husband through their rough patch. She seemed receptive and willing. It was only a short interaction, but God put it on the list of specific assignments he had just for me. I still think of that woman from time to time and hope she and her husband are doing well.

Another situation came about from my familiarity with and recent journey through grief. My husband and I lost our second daughter the year prior, when I was seven months pregnant with her. While it was the most devastating experience we had ever been through, God, in his grace and kindness, used us to help others through their grief. In the ED, one of our nurses found herself grieving the loss of her first granddaughter, who was stillborn. She was in the delivery room and tried everything to try to help revive her. She, her daughter, and her son-in-law experienced excruciating emotional pain. I was privileged to hug them, cry with them, and pray with them. As we looked at pictures together, we shared our questions of how we would go on without these precious little girls, but we knew they were with Jesus.

A third situation was when I was able to walk beside a fellow nurse through a battle with cancer. She was very young yet had an aggressive and debilitating cancer. Through the help of my dad and his prayer partner, we were able to pray with her often and encourage her. Her cancer went into remission while I was still working in the ED. It did eventually come back, and she lost her battle, but I am thankful to the Lord I was there during those first months.

The fourth situation is probably the most meaningful to me because it brought closure and beauty to a ten-year-old relationship. When I was a newly graduated nurse, I worked on the busiest cardiac floor of the hospital. One of the more seasoned nurses had absolutely no use for me. She seemed to make a sport of leaving my questions unanswered, making snide comments, and basically watching me flounder if I needed help. She eventually softened and one day asked me out on one of her smoke breaks and told me all about her cats and her strained relationship with her mother. After that bonding experience, we were able to work together in a much healthier way. I moved floors not long after that and did not see her again until one day in the ED. We got a call that a nurse from one of the floors was experiencing a significant medical event that usually had poor outcomes. Once I received the name, I quickly made my way to the room. I bent over her bed and told her I was there with her. She looked up at me and called me the ridiculous nickname she had for me when we worked together, and we both had a laugh. I then was able to pray with her before the helicopter came to fly her north to receive higher-level care. She lived through the life-threatening event, and I was so grateful. I was also thankful that she and the other nurses in the room that day heard us turn to God. After all, he deserved the glory for saving her life that day.

While these four stories might make it seem that all my time in the ED was completely redeemed, that is not the case. I wish I could say my attitude always rose to match the redemptive work God was doing there. Truthfully, however, I found myself complaining often. There were other times I tried to work out God's will for him, and at a faster pace than he seemed to be working! All in all, it was a long two years. The job-sharing situation never got better, so I just did my best. Looking back, I am so grateful that God still chose to use me, reveal some of his ways to me, and teach me that trusting him is always the ultimate goal in any and every situation.

Those experiences showed me that persistence means showing up, even in hard circumstances. Persistence means surrendering myself to God's will, ways, and plans, even when they are unclear in the moment. Persistence means looking up, when I am stuck, to a loving and sovereign God who has more than my own best interests at heart. He wants to use me to bring about his best plans for those around me too!

I was eventually released by the Lord to leave that position after those two years. I returned to teaching and never returned to hospital work. But those two years were not wasted. God works everything "together for good to them that love God" and "are the called according to *his* purpose" (Romans 8:28, KJV).

TIFFANY GREER *was born and raised in Park Forest, Illinois. She earned a BSN from Olivet and a PhD in nursing education from Capella University. She joined the Olivet nursing faculty in 2002, teaching didactic and clinical nursing courses. She began serving as the associate dean of the School of Nursing in 2016 and is presently pursuing ordination in the Church of the Nazarene. Tiffany and her husband, Mitch, have a daughter and a son.*

HITTING THE WALL
Dale Hathaway

We all tend to gravitate toward subjects and areas of interest that come easily for us. Perhaps nowhere is this more evident than on a university campus. For example, if you have a knack for picking up other languages, you may major in Spanish or French, or something even more exotic. If you have good eye-hand coordination, you may participate in athletic events like baseball, softball, or basketball. If you have an ability to pick up a musical instrument and make pleasing sounds, you may consider a music major. This behavior is natural and part of what we all do as humans: we play to our strengths.

But what do you do when your strength in an area is not enough? How do you handle that change, and how do you move forward? Or, more generally, what do you do if you have been able to do well in a subject but suddenly that easy subject becomes hard? That is what this story is about.

Math always came easy to me; it was my area of strength. I naturally think logically and typically pay attention to small details. I grew up in a household where both my parents were teachers. My mom taught first grade, and my dad taught high school math, so I suppose it is not surprising that mathematics came easy to me. When it came time for college, I only applied to one school—Eastern Nazarene College (ENC), the school my parents and older sisters had attended.

At ENC I knew I would major in mathematics, but I also considered chemistry and computer science. After struggling with the chemistry labs in the spring semester of my freshman year, I eliminated that option. The computer science program was just being developed at that time, so I kept pursuing that option along with the easy and natural option of mathematics. During my junior, year I dropped the computer science major to have more time to be involved in student government (in hindsight, that may not have been the best choice).

While I was in college, some subjects I studied were very challenging. For instance, when I took the required general education history course, I would start studying on Monday for a Friday exam, putting in several hours of study every day in preparation for the upcoming test. It did not come easy to me, so I had to work hard to reach the level of achievement I desired. Mathematics, on the other hand, was easy for me. I rarely had to put in significant chunks of time for a math exam. I still remember a differential equations exam when the professor was not there, and he had a student proctor the exam who happened to be a friend of mine. I will always remember the look of shock on my friend's face when I turned in my exam, which was scheduled for the full sixty-five-minute class period, after only about fifteen minutes. I think I received a score of 98 percent on that exam. Looking back, I would add that it is not that big of a deal to perform well on things that come easy to us. The true measure is what we do when easy things become difficult.

As my college career wound down, I decided to apply to grad school. Ultimately, I settled on Boston University, largely for geographical reasons: I was already familiar with the Boston area. I was a little concerned about whether I was truly ready for graduate work in mathematics, but I had breezed through every course I had taken in college, so I figured things would work out.

I was a teaching assistant, so I was expected to help professors with their lower-level math courses. As a result, I was only allowed to take a maximum of five courses per year. Wanting to get the most out of the courses I was allowed to take, for that first semester I signed up for the following three: Numerical Analysis, Operations Research, and Introduction to Analysis I. The first exam rolled around in Introduction to Analysis I. I prepared for it just like I prepared for all my previous college-level math courses, and when I got the graded exam back a few weeks later, I had earned a 67 percent. I had never received lower than a B on a math exam before—much less a D. In a graduate-level course, I needed a B or better just to get credit, and I was nowhere close to that level of achievement. I had hit the wall.

We all hit the wall at some point—where what has previously come easy suddenly becomes challenging. Grad-school mathematics was so much more difficult for me than undergrad math. I had a decision to make: give up because it was no longer easy (like I had done with chemistry), or change how I approached my preparation for classes and exams. I chose to change my approach. I started spending more time on really understanding the material, and I purchased other books on the subject to see if they would give me additional insight. On a few occasions, I actually went and asked my professors questions. If I wanted to make math my career, I needed to be willing to put in the extra work to ensure I could succeed and that my understanding was accurate.

When you hit the wall—when a subject or activity that once was easy is unexpectedly challenging—you have a choice to make. If what you have been doing is no longer leading to a successful outcome, you may have to change how you approach things in order to achieve success. In academics, this might mean spending more time on a subject than you previously needed, and possibly more time than you spend on other subjects. It might mean doing things you did not need to do in the past. Do not let this deter you. New situations often call for new approaches. If you want to succeed, you may need to get extra help or find additional resources related to the topic.

Let me repeat that we all hit the wall at some point. The issue is not when it happens so much as how we respond. The when is irrelevant. Some students hit the wall in high school and some in early college, while others hit the wall in upper-division courses. The important question is not when but how. How will we respond? Will we be stubborn, refusing to change how we approach things, even though our approach no longer leads to success? Or will we acknowledge that what worked in the past does not seem to be enough anymore and a different approach is needed?

Choosing the latter option prepares us for a life that will sometimes throw challenges at us along the way. Being willing to change our approach will not guarantee success or that things will be easy, but it will ensure a healthy degree of flexibility in how adversity is handled. Furthermore, such an approach provides a path more likely to lead to future success.

DALE HATHAWAY *was born and raised in Connecticut. He earned a BS in mathematics from Eastern Nazarene College and a PhD in mathematics from Boston University. He joined the Olivet faculty in 1989 and has taught mathematics and served as a department chair. He currently serves as the associate dean of the Martin D. Walker School of STEM. Dale and his wife, Heather, have three adult children.*

11
RED 54
Bruce Heyen

My eyes focused on the handwritten 54. That was the number written in red ink glaring at me on the paper with my name on it. As a first-year chemistry graduate student, I stared at the number incredulously, but it did not change! That red number was my percentage grade on one of the first exams I took in grad school. Adding insult to injury, this particular assessment had been an open-note exam. My next thoughts logically spiraled down to negative self-talk: *Who knows how poorly I might have done without my notes since I could not even pass the exam with notes?* A failing grade in the class most certainly meant I would struggle to stay in grad school.

Almost immediately, and for weeks after that red-number event, doubts about my choice to attend grad school crept into my mind. Now what was I supposed to do? I had prepared for this opportunity with years of rigorous undergraduate work. Was this now a reflection of my inadequate preparation? A host of other questions assaulted me:

Am I cut out for graduate work?

Why have I moved away from home just to fail?

Do I belong with my fellow students, who also worked countless hours to get to this school?

Do I even like chemistry?

Am I smart enough?

Can I endure four years of this level of rigor to get a PhD?

Are grad school and a career in chemistry God's plan for me?

Can I persist?

These questions and more raged through my mind as I contemplated my future plans. I began doing some soul searching.

What else could I do with my life?

Maybe I should try to get a master's degree in chemistry instead of a PhD—or find a job that doesn't require an advanced degree at all.

Maybe I should have majored in something else.

One of my personal challenges in life has been having diverse interests in so many subjects. I was an accomplished musician, and was especially drawn to church music, so I wondered about pursuing a career as a music pastor. Then I thought about getting a master's degree in education, being done with grad school in a few years, and teaching at a high school. I also thought about pursuing bachelor's-level jobs in the chemical industry. I actually researched all of these options seriously and sought counsel and wisdom from my peers, family, and friends. I visited seminaries. I visited schools of education. My desire to persist on my current trajectory was being called into question.

In the meantime, I kept plugging away at my coursework, hoping to improve my exam scores, but I was struggling to maintain the motivation needed. Several of my other courses were difficult as well, and my soul and brain were weary. I had been taking exams and going to school for eighteen years by the time I reached grad school. Due to a significant change in my college major, I found myself on the five-year plan as an undergraduate student. Did I now want to extend the rigors even further?

Furthermore, the career crisis was not the only event in my grad-school experience that made me question where my life was headed. I was the victim of a major bicycle accident on campus that left me with a severely crushed finger on my dominant piano-playing right hand. The accident required surgery and five pins. Then my research proposal was rejected by my faculty committee, requiring me to start over with a completely new proposal on an entirely different subject. At the same time, one of my committee members was the victim of a bomb threat that made national news. I feared it may have put him in a bad mood, thus increasing the general anxiety I was experiencing with my committee and proposal at the time. In addition to everything else, I lived far from my hometown and had to miss the funeral of a young cousin; my parents were pressuring my wife and me to attend a different church; and I was grilled by a job recruiter and then not offered the job I wanted. Life was difficult.

While I could easily dwell on all these negative events, I must admit there were definitely some positive things that happened during grad school too. I had a close-knit research group and a supportive advisor. My wife was offered a nursing job at the hospital of her choice. The church we attended gave us opportunities for music ministry, and we developed some lifelong friendships there with fellow members who became surrogate parents to us since we were far from home. Our first child was born. My thesis defense went smoothly. My wife and I had many reasons to be thankful to God and enjoy his blessings.

Through all my soul searching about whether to continue in grad school, one thought kept running through my mind: if I had the ability to keep diligently working, and if I truly was able to complete grad school with God's help, the end result would be totally worth the effort. I wanted to teach at the college level, and this was the route I needed to take to accomplish that career goal. So I persevered and completed my PhD in just over four years, one full week before I began my first college teaching job. While I know I probably could have chosen other careers and been successful, God has given me gifts to use and joys to share in my chosen profession.

As it turned out, the grade of 54 that began my existential crisis was the average for that class. Average! Discovering that I was average was a source of comfort. It meant I had scored in the middle of my cohort rather than at the lower end. I would, of course, much rather have been in the top third. But it helped me realize I had the ability to succeed in grad school, just not always at the level of my high expectations. I did end up with a B in the course, and that was good enough for this persevering student.

Thank you, Lord, for giving me the ability to persist so I could spend my career sharing my passion for teaching and chemistry.

BRUCE HEYEN *was born and raised on a farm in south-central Kansas. He earned his BS in biochemistry from Abilene Christian University and his PhD in chemistry from Northwestern University. In 2016 he joined the faculty at Olivet, where he teaches chemistry and serves as chair of the Department of Chemistry and Geosciences. Bruce and his wife, Janell, have five children and two grandchildren scattered coast to coast and across the world.*

STRESSED AND SLEEPLESS
Ryan Himes

I wanted to give up. I wanted to give up on my career. I even thought about giving up on God. It was the spring of 2012, and I was nearing the end of the second year in my PhD program.

I had been a strong student for years leading up to this season in my life. I started taking my education seriously during high school, and in college I pushed myself to do my best, even in some very challenging courses. My Christian college professors were wonderful, inspiring me to try to become a professor myself one day, but I knew that would require earning a PhD. After I earned my bachelor's degree in 2006, I took a few years away from school to work in a science research lab, then entered a PhD program in 2010.

I did well in the first three semesters of that program, but during the fourth semester it seemed like everything was about to fall apart. I was busy working on research for my dissertation and was scheduled to give a presentation of my progress to a group of professors and other scientists at the beginning of May. A week after that, I would have to take final exams for two tough courses: neurobiology and a med-school-level human physiology class. As if all that weren't daunting enough, I was preparing in advance for June, when I would have to sit for my qualifying exams.

In a science doctoral program, you must pass qualifying exams to be considered a true PhD candidate. If you pass, you can continue in the program; if you don't pass, your professors have the option to dismiss you. In my program, the qualifying exams included coming up with a proposal for a brand-new scientific research project, presenting that proposal to a panel of professors, and then answering the professors' questions. Their questions could be about any aspect of the proposal—or anything else that I had been taught in my first two years of graduate school.

It was an extremely stressful time, to say the least. Though I tried to prepare for these three major tasks—my dissertation, major course exams, and the qualifying exams—I was increasingly filled with anxiety. When May arrived, it was time for me to present my dissertation research. I actually thought this would be the least difficult of the tasks because I enjoyed public speaking, and my research had been going well. But right after my presentation, my neurobiology professor, who would also be on the panel judging my qualifying exams, said something like, "If you perform on your qualifying exams the way you just performed in that presentation, you should expect to fail."

It's difficult to express in words how anxious her warning made me feel. I was working as hard as I could, and I thought I had just delivered an excellent presentation, yet she thought it was so poor that I deserved to fail! How was I ever going to pass my qualifying exams? What was I going to do with my life after failing in grad school? What would my family and friends think of me if my career fell apart with no backup plan in place? And how would I ever be a provider for my family?

Around this same time, my wife of four years became pregnant for the first time, but she experienced a devastating miscarriage—the hardest thing we had yet gone through in our young marriage. Now I was not only dealing with the stress and anxiety of potentially failing out of grad school, but my wife and I were also working through serious emotional pain.

Eventually, all the anxiety, pain, and stress reached a peak and erupted like a volcano. I was studying for my final exams in neurobiology and physiology, and my anxiety level was so high that I couldn't sleep that night. The next day, I tried to continue studying, but I was so tired from lack of sleep that it wasn't going well. Still, I couldn't sleep because my heart was racing. When I couldn't sleep for the second night in a row, I started to panic. How was I supposed to study and prepare properly if I couldn't concentrate and couldn't sleep?

The experience really tested my faith. I began asking myself, *Do I truly believe in God? Do I really trust that God is with me and can help me through this?* I felt like I was facing a choice: I could either surrender to my doubt and conclude that God wasn't real and that I was on my own to navigate my life and career. Or I could put my faith in God once again and trust him for my next steps.

I chose to believe in God's promise: "I will never desert you, nor will I ever abandon you" (Hebrews 13:5b, NASB). I couldn't prove it, but I wondered if perhaps God was trying to tell me, *"You're not alone. I have always been with you, and I am with you now. I am strong, and I will walk along this difficult path with you."* I made the decision to put my faith in God. I determined that, if God was with me, I would take one step of faith after another and keep trusting him.

As a first step, I sought medical attention for my anxiety attack. I was prescribed some anti-anxiety medication, which helped me calm down enough to get some sleep. But that alone wouldn't enable me to pass my finals and my qualifying exams. The finals were only two days away. For the next step, I used the remaining time to study as much as I could, and I passed the exams!

Now that the second task was complete, I had one month to get ready for the daunting qualifying exams. I set a weekly schedule for how I would prepare, but I limited myself to no more than eight hours of studying per day. I knew I would need time each day to take care of myself (including sleep, prayer, and exercise), plus a Sabbath each week for rest. I added those priorities to my schedule. I also wanted to continue investing in my marriage and in our church community that was supporting us as we continued to grieve the miscarriage. Limiting my daily study time and scheduling these other priorities was an act of faith. If I was truly going to trust God, I couldn't make an idol out of my qualifying exams. I needed to put my relationship with God first, followed by my marriage, my community of support, and my own health. All of these were more important than successfully finishing a PhD program.

That next month was probably the toughest month of my life. There were many times when it would have been easier just to give up and quit grad school. But I persevered and stuck to my schedule. As the day of my qualifying exams drew near, I felt more confident that I could pass. I also grew stronger in my faith in God as I sensed him helping me along. My marriage likewise grew stronger during this time as my wife supported me in my study and preparation. Together, we began to heal from the pain of the miscarriage.

Well, you know what happened, or else I wouldn't be writing this today as a college professor: I passed my qualifying exams, and I completed my PhD three years later. Right when I was finishing, a job opened at Olivet for a professor of physiology. I've now been teaching this subject to undergraduate students for the past decade, and I love doing it.

With God's gracious and faithful help, I made it through the darkest time in my life. While I didn't want to go through all that, now that I'm on the other side, I'm a stronger person with a stronger marriage and a deeper faith. For that I'm grateful. I'm grateful that God helped me persist so I could teach at Olivet. I'm grateful that I've been able to draw on these personal experiences when counseling numerous Olivet students who experience anxiety and doubt. And I'll be even more grateful if God continues to use my story to encourage readers like you.

RYAN HIMES *grew up in Elmhurst, Illinois. He earned his BS in chemistry from Wheaton College and his PhD in physiology from Loyola University Chicago. He joined Olivet's faculty in 2015 as a professor of biological sciences. He and his wife, Sarah, have two daughters.*

AIRPORT TEARS AND DESPAIR
Andrew Hoag

I didn't have crying in the middle of an airport bathroom on my 2014 bingo card. Yet that's where I found myself in November of that year.

I was at the San Diego airport preparing to fly to San Antonio, Texas, to defend my doctoral dissertation at The University of Texas at San Antonio. This journey represented the culmination of four and a half years of PhD work, research, and two moves between California and Texas. At the same time, my wife, Brenda, was pregnant with our first child. This latter development was also four years in the making, due to unexplained infertility. These simultaneous efforts—completing my PhD and beginning our family—took tremendous amounts of prayer, patience, and, yes, persistence. So, why was I, on the precipice of achieving both of those goals, crying in the San Diego airport bathroom?

A few days before my flight, Brenda and I received a follow-up phone call from her OB/GYN after her twenty-week pregnancy scan. They saw potential signs of vasa previa, a rare condition in which the umbilical cord lacks the membrane that protects the blood vessels inside, making it susceptible to rupture, which would endanger both mother and baby. For four years, we had gone to doctors, prayed, cried, held each other, and hoped to have a child to hold in our arms. Now, halfway through my wife's first pregnancy, we faced the possibility of losing our son.

With our hopes crashing against the mountainside of despair, I had to leave my wife by herself and fly to San Antonio to complete the most important moment of my professional career to that point. During the days before the trip, I comforted Brenda, edited the PowerPoint for my defense, and packed for the days I would be gone—activities that enabled me to hold the despair at bay. My pause in the airport bathroom was the first time I had stopped moving in days, and the floodgates opened.

Persistence is a concept with which I feel well acquainted. Anyone who goes through four years of college, two years of a master's program, and four and a half years of PhD work has to be particularly adept at sticking with things. Even in our relationship, Brenda and I persisted through two years of long-distance dating while I was at Point Loma Nazarene University before she transferred down to join me. Then, through our four-year infertility journey, I was often the one to keep the level head and articulate our hopes that God would hear our prayers for a child. I've tried hard most of my life to be the tree that bends but doesn't break against the winds of life.

The hurricane of that week in November, however, threatened to break me for the first time in my life. I wish I could say I made it through that dark season due entirely to my own effort and innate ability to persist, but I'm not that strong. While the doctoral defense was successful and I was officially Dr. Hoag, the weight of that despair continued to crush me. I learned quickly that finishing the PhD was just the start of my career, not any sort of ending worth dwelling on. Now I had to begin the journey toward a full-time professor position, a journey I had no way of knowing would take six years of twists and turns before I ended up at Olivet.

More importantly, I couldn't shake the terrible knowledge that there was little—if anything—I could do to protect my wife and son from the dangers of that diagnosis. Vasa previa isn't guaranteed to be fatal, but my words of hope and optimism quickly lost their strength when Brenda's college roommate—a nurse with an irrepressibly sunny disposition—responded to the news with a deflating, "Oh no, Bren! That's awful!" When a labor-and-delivery nurse starts with a statement like that in response to your diagnosis, no words and will to persist can keep you afloat. Despair threatened to make that moment of crying uncontrollably in an airport bathroom my new default emotional state.

What got us out of that pit? What compelled us to persist? I promise you that it was no effort of our own or of anyone else. It was God, pure and simple. Brenda's OB recommended her to a specialist who could use more high-tech equipment to better diagnose the problem, but we were sent to this specialist with the warning that vasa previa was the likely diagnosis and that our best-case scenario was two to three months of bed rest and an early C-section to save both Brenda and our son.

After three weeks of waiting, we went to the specialist. Then, after about five minutes of him checking our son with his fancy ultrasound machine, he reinflated our hopes with a perfunctory, "Well, looks good!" Noticing our disbelief, he explained further: "The umbilical cord is fine. No vasa previa." The problem was gone. We received no definitive explanation of what may have happened. Either the umbilical cord had always been fine, or it had miraculously regrown the membrane that usually covers and protects the blood vessels from damage.

Of course, we recognize the possibility—maybe a likelihood—that the original diagnosis was wrong, but Brenda and I think it is equally possible that there was, in fact, something wrong and that God healed the problem. Whether God redeemed the physical situation or not, the real miracle is how he healed our hearts. The prospect of losing the baby we had strived for over the course of four years threatened to destroy us, and God redeemed us from that valley of despair! In the midst of the darkness that threatened to swallow us, God's light shined through and reminded us that he was with us in all things.

Our first child, Oliver Vance Hoag, was born healthy on March 19, 2015. Our blessings from God didn't end there; in fact, the next blessing came a lot sooner than expected when our second child, Everett, arrived on April 21, 2016. That's right! We went from wondering if we would ever have a child, to fearing we would lose our baby, to then having two children under the age of two. Believe me when I say that Brenda and I learned a different, more joyful lesson about persistence during that chaotic but wonderful season. Fortunately, the final blessing in our family waited four years to arrive. Our third child, Vivienne, was born in March 2020, the day after California issued shelter-in-place orders for the COVID-19 pandemic.

That moment of our daughter's birth crystallized in my mind what God has taught me in the time since November 2014: during any difficulty—whether infertility or a pandemic—God is working and blessing us in amazing ways that maybe we don't always notice in the moment. When we feared for the life of our unborn son and were uncertain what my academic career would look like, we had no idea God was preparing us for the incredible life we have here at Olivet with our three children. Beyond that, God was developing in us the fruit of the Spirit through these trials. As Paul writes in Galatians 5, we needed the Spirit's "love, joy, peace, forbearance, kindness, goodness, faithfulness, gentleness and self-control" (vv. 22–23) to survive these trying circumstances.

Without the gift of God's presence in our lives, we would have drowned in our despair. But with his Spirit guiding us by the hand, we could persist in all things. I didn't know what God was doing in my life in that low moment in the San Diego airport bathroom, but with hindsight I know that God didn't forsake me. He had plans for my benefit. I've had other hard days since then, and many more tears, but I'll never forget how God met me in that moment and kept me on the path he has set before me. All he asks of me is to trust in him and keep walking on that path.

ANDREW HOAG *was born and raised in Arroyo Grande, California. He earned a BA from Point Loma Nazarene University and a PhD in English from The University of Texas at San Antonio. A member of Olivet's faculty since 2020, he teaches writing courses in the Department of English. Andrew and his wife, Brenda, have three children.*

THE DECISION
Dave Horton

Life was good. My wife and I had built our dream home in a western suburb of Detroit, adopted our oldest son, and had a church we loved with a wonderful group of friends. We had settled into a routine and were enjoying our lives.

However, I was feeling restless at work. I had been a manager at the IRS for nine years and was ready to move on. I had always wanted to be an executive and still felt that was what I needed to do. The next step in that process was to become a senior manager. The obstacle to obtaining a senior manager position in the Detroit area was the current senior manager, who was not interested in moving up to an executive position. She was at least ten years from retirement, and that was longer than I wanted to wait to become a senior manager so I could eventually become an executive.

That meant I needed to look for opportunities outside the Detroit area. My wife was not excited. We spent hours discussing the possibility. She had worked at the same hospital since graduating from Olivet and had moved into a corporate administrative position. She loved what she was doing, and there was a daycare at the hospital. Our son was thriving, and he was being well cared for while we both worked.

After much discussion and praying for guidance, we decided I should start applying for senior manager positions when they became available. Two opportunities surfaced. One was in Pittsburgh, Pennsylvania, and the other was in Jacksonville, Florida. We looked at both cities carefully. I was temporarily covering as the senior manager in Pittsburgh at the time, so we were able to look at Pittsburgh closely. Pittsburgh is hilly, and my wife has bad knees, so that was going to be a significant challenge for her if we moved there. She spent two days with a real estate agent and did not find a single house that she could live in because they were all built into hillsides with one or two flights of stairs. Navigating those steps on a daily basis had no appeal. Neither of us had been to Jacksonville before, but we could easily find dozens of one-story homes with flat backyards in a brief internet search. After careful consideration, we decided I should apply for both positions and tell them that Jacksonville was my preference.

I was offered both positions and accepted the one in Jacksonville without having ever been there to look for a house. As we started preparing to move, my wife tried to resign from the hospital. Surprisingly, her boss would not let her quit. Instead, my wife's supervisor gave her a laptop and made her job remote. In 2004, working from home was not an option for most people, especially in nursing positions. Yet she worked for the hospital all the years we lived in Jacksonville.

The hardest part of leaving Michigan was saying goodbye to our friends and family in the Midwest. We had a wonderful group of friends at Detroit First Church of the Nazarene, where we taught the college and career Sunday school class. I was the church treasurer, and my wife was helping with women's ministries. Both of our parents were in Michigan, and siblings were only a few hours away. Our friends had walked through several difficult life challenges with us. We had shared joys and sorrows with them, loved their children, and were looking forward to our son having the opportunity to get to know them and grow up in their presence. It broke our hearts to leave them.

We made the 1,200-mile journey to Jacksonville. After getting settled, we found a local church plant whose co-pastors had graduated from Olivet with me. We watched the church grow, and I had the opportunity to assist in getting the financing in place so their own facility could be built. We also met a family through the preschool our son attended. They had adopted three times and were in the process of doing so again. They introduced us to their attorney, and we decided to start the adoption process again ourselves. We adopted our second son while we were in Jacksonville.

I loved my job. I was responsible for all the large-corporation audits in Florida except for the Miami/Fort Lauderdale area. The position required that I travel more than we had anticipated, including several temporary assignments in Washington, DC. After three years in Jacksonville, I applied for the executive program and was selected to begin my first executive job in the Chicago area, which of course meant another relocation.

After moving to Oswego, a far western suburb of Chicago, I started my executive journey at the IRS. In my first assignment, my former senior manager from Detroit worked for me. She and I had a great working relationship. We even taught a workshop about "how to raise your boss" after we swapped positions. I ended up holding four distinct executive positions in the Chicago area until I went to Washington, DC, to become the deputy commissioner and then acting commissioner of the Tax-Exempt Government Entities division. I had never imagined working at that level.

We really missed our friends from Detroit. Most of them made the trip to Florida at least once during the three and a half years we lived there, and most years we saw them at Christmastime when we traveled back for the holidays. After we moved to the Chicago area, friends from Detroit approached us about purchasing their summer cottage at the Indian Lake Nazarene Campground near Kalamazoo, Michigan. It seemed like a perfect halfway point between Chicago and Detroit. We bought their wonderful cottage, and my wife would take our boys there on the same day school got out for the summer and stay until just a day or two before school started in Illinois. Later, some of our other friends started purchasing campground cottages and lakefront homes there as well. Eventually, we had influenced eleven families to join us at the campground. Our boys ended up getting to spend their summers with the friends we loved so much after all. And some of our campground friends are now those married couples, and their children, from the college and career Sunday school class we taught during our early years in Detroit.

We have been in Oswego for the past seventeen years and have managed to put both of our boys through school from kindergarten to high school in the same school district with the same neighborhood friends. Prior to moving back to the Midwest, we moved every three to five years. But had we not moved to Florida, I would not have reached the executive level of leadership within the IRS, which is what eventually enabled us to give our boys a consistent location in which to grow up.

As difficult as the original decision was, we are so grateful we made it. We would never have adopted our second son, we would have missed the opportunity to participate in a church plant, and we would have been unlikely to celebrate the reunion of our friends at Indian Lake. As I look back on all of it, I am reminded of God's faithfulness to guide our paths when we persist in following him.

DAVE HORTON *was raised in Port Huron, Michigan. He earned a BS from Olivet and an MS in taxation from Walsh College. Dave joined the Olivet faculty in 2021 after a long career working for the IRS. He teaches accounting courses in Olivet's McGraw School of Business. Dave and his wife, Sandy, have two sons.*

PREPARATION MADE THE DIFFERENCE
Dave Johnson

In August 2009, I was about to take my PhD candidacy exams at Northern Illinois University. I had completed all my coursework, and successfully passing my two candidacy exams would mean I could move on to the dissertation stage of the program. I would be one step closer to earning my degree and continuing my career and calling as an English professor.

Honestly, though, I did not prepare as well as I should have for the exams. In the months leading up to them, I had been busy with my full-time job teaching at Olivet and balancing a number of major life events, some wonderful and some heartbreaking. In March of that year, I asked the love of my life to marry me, and we were excitedly preparing for our wedding later that fall. But my parents lived more than a thousand miles away in Florida, and my father had spent the past year battling for his life after receiving a diagnosis of acute myeloid leukemia. By the time of my exams, my dad was not doing well at all.

The day for my first candidacy exam arrived. I had four hours to answer three questions related to my selected field of British literature since 1900. Immediately upon seeing the prompts, I knew I was in trouble. I *might* be able to write passable answers for two of the questions, but I had absolutely no idea how to answer the third. I knew I was sunk. Two days later, I was seated once again at the university's testing center to complete my second candidacy exam, this time in my other selected field, American literature since 1865. This exam went well enough, and I felt I had done alright, but I was performing under dark mental and emotional clouds.

I would have to wait a few weeks for the official decision, but I was certain I had not passed the first candidacy exam. However, I did not have time to dwell on it; my fiancée, Val, and I flew to Florida the day after that second exam to visit my parents. I spent almost the entire trip sitting by my father's bedside as he struggled through the last days of his life. I was simultaneously blessed and heartbroken to be with him as he took his final breaths before entering his heavenly home.

The next few weeks were a blur: helping my mother with funeral preparations, trying to get my ONU classes launched, helping Val with final wedding arrangements. Then I received the letter from NIU that confirmed my suspicions. I had passed one candidacy exam and failed the other. I would have one opportunity to retake the exam I had failed, but if I did not pass a second time, I would be at risk of being expelled from the program.

Failing the exam was a major wakeup call. I knew that literary studies and teaching at the college level were my calling. God had been faithful to me on every single step of my journey. For my part, I had always given my best effort teaching my classes at Olivet and working on the PhD at NIU—up until those candidacy exams, that is. Yes, I was in a season full of wonderful and heartbreaking life events, but the fact remained: I had not prepared properly, and now it was possible I might fail out of my doctoral program.

However, the journey was not over yet, and God certainly was not done teaching me about his faithfulness and provision. With renewed resolve and determination, I started preparing to retake the exam I had failed. NIU offered the exams twice a year, once in December and once in August. Realistically, I knew I would not be ready in time to retake the exam that December. This meant I would have to wait until the following August, but it also gave me more time to focus and prepare.

I reached out to one of my professors at NIU (who would soon become my dissertation advisor), and he began mentoring me for the exam. He sent me to the library, where I could view earlier versions of the candidacy exams. Based on those earlier exams and Dr. Baker's recommendations, I researched, read, and took notes. Once every week or two, I sat down for four hours to write essay responses to the old exams. Week after week (after week) I did this, and week after week (after week), Dr. Baker provided me with feedback on each practice exam I wrote. Dr. Baker was the answer to my prayers. He came along at just the time that I needed someone who could see the situation more clearly than I could and who could guide and encourage me where I needed it most. Between God's faithfulness, Dr. Baker's mentorship, and the hard work I was putting in, I gained confidence that I would pass the exam.

The day for the exam arrived. My wife dropped me off at the testing center. Immediately upon seeing the prompts, I knew I would do well. Even before typing a word, I mentally envisioned how I would craft each essay in response to questions for which I was well prepared. The next four hours flew by, and when my wife picked me up and asked how it had gone, I could not suppress my smile.

Again, it would be a few weeks before I received the official decision, but this time I waited with eagerness rather than dread. The letter from NIU soon arrived and again confirmed my suspicion: I had passed. Not only had I passed; I had passed with distinction, which is the highest mark possible on a candidacy exam. God had demonstrated his faithfulness one more time. He blessed the hard work I had put in to preparing for the retake, and he blessed me with wise and encouraging mentorship from Dr. Baker. As a result of God's faithfulness and blessing, I was able to continue and eventually complete my doctorate in English.

DAVE JOHNSON *was born and raised in St. Louis, Missouri, and has been a lifelong fan of the St. Louis Cardinals. He earned his BA from Olivet and his PhD in English from Northern Illinois University. He joined the faculty in 2002 and teaches literature in the Department of English. Dave and his wife, Val, have two daughters.*

FROM POVERTY TO PROFESSOR
Marvin Jones

I was raised in a little house on Albemarle Avenue in Waynesboro, Virginia. At the most, it might have been five hundred square feet. There were four rooms: two bedrooms, a kitchen, and a living room. The living room and kitchen each had a gas stove holding four bricks to heat the entire house, though the size of the house made that not a very big task. We had no running water, no bathroom, and barely enough room for our family consisting of eight children and Mom.

Of the four rooms that made up the house, the front bedroom was occupied by Mom. We kids slept in the back bedroom, where we shared a queen-size bed and a set of bunk beds. As I got older, I eventually began sleeping on the sofa in the living room.

Our paternal grandparents lived across the street. That is where I went to get our water. I would take a five-gallon, galvanized bucket to their home and fill it so we could have water to drink. In the summer, flies were so bad in the house that we had to cover the bucket with a tea towel and then spray insecticide.

My parents divorced when I was very young, so Mom was left to raise us pretty much on her own. For a while, she worked at our town hospital, serving as a cook in the kitchen. Mom was a wonderful cook. During the week, we ate whatever we could find, but on Sunday, Mom made us fried chicken, green beans, macaroni and cheese, and homemade hot rolls. We looked forward to those Sunday meals. There were times we did not have much to eat, so I would go four houses down the road to my great-grandmother's house to see if she had anything for me to make a sandwich. I often found some cabbage that had turned a light brown color because it had been cooking on a woodburning stove all day long. It was the best-tasting cabbage I have ever had to this day.

A government program offered monthly food commodities. As the oldest boy, I had the job of going with Mom to pick up the food. When I got old enough, I went alone. It was embarrassing to have to live on government commodities, though we looked forward to the beginning of the month, when we knew it was time to get that food. In the box were government cheese (still the best cheese in the world, in my opinion), canned meat that they said was pork (doubtful), butter, puffed wheat cereal, canned green beans, powdered milk, oatmeal, and other items I can no longer remember. That box of food was the only thing that kept us from being without at times.

When it was time for us to take baths, I would carry water from my grandparents' house across the street to fill a large tub that was placed in the middle of the kitchen. We took turns, and the goal was to be first in the tub so we could get fresh, clean water. When it was time to use the bathroom, we walked the path behind the house to the outhouse. We did this in both winter and summer.

Somewhere along the line, I subconsciously decided that if I ever had children, they would not have to live this way. Those experiences motivated me, at the age of thirteen, to become a little entrepreneur. Whenever I needed or wanted anything, since there was no extra money, I began going from business to business in the downtown area, where I asked if I could wash their windows, help with the cleaning, or do whatever task they needed. I did this so I could have some of the things I needed and wanted. I secured two paper routes: one in the morning for *The Richmond Times Dispatch* and one in the afternoon for *The News Virginian*. I also worked on Saturdays at a local car wash, where I received not only a small wage but also tips from the customers if I did a good job.

Once I got to high school, I was selected to sing in the school's concert choir. To be in the choir, however, I had to purchase a dinner jacket. The cost was astronomical for a kid like me: seventy-five dollars. If I were ever to get a jacket, I knew I would have to be the one to buy it. So, along with all the other part-time jobs I had, I began singing in local bands on the weekend.

College was nothing but a far-off dream for me. Quite honestly, I knew we could not afford it; I also never thought I was smart enough. Most of my friends and a couple of my cousins went to college, but I did not. I got married twenty days after graduating from high school and began to work, trying to make a decent living. Getting a job was never difficult, but no matter how much money I made, it never seemed to be enough. I had a great work ethic that served me well.

Over time, I eventually became a Christ follower and began singing in churches. I sensed a call to ministry and followed that call, entering the Course of Study program offered by the Church of the Nazarene. I was ordained as an elder in 1991.

My full-time ministry began in two church communities in Virginia before moving to a church in Nashville, Tennessee. The Nashville opportunity was located on a college campus, so while I was there—at the age of thirty-seven—I began working on a bachelor's degree in church music. The degree took me nine years to complete. By the time I graduated, I was the first member of my family to complete a college degree.

Several years later, in 2006, I began a graduate program in religion with a focus on preaching. That period was a great time of study for me. I enjoyed it immensely and graduated with my master's degree in 2009. Never in a million years would I have dreamed that I, a boy from what today would be labeled "the projects" of Waynesboro, Virginia, would graduate with a master's degree in religion and have the opportunities I then had in life. Of course, the entire time I was in school, I still had to care for my family and keep showing up at my job to support them. To say I was busy would be an understatement. I was burning the candle at both ends. Yet there was satisfaction in knowing I had accomplished something no one else in my family had accomplished at the time.

After completing my master's degree, I worked three more years before, out of the blue, I decided to apply to a doctoral program. Secretly, I had always wanted to have a doctorate. However, I had an honorary doctorate in mind because I never thought I would be able to do the academic work required to earn one otherwise.

The admissions committee, to my surprise, accepted me into the EdD program in 2012. I was ecstatic as I began the journey toward my doctoral degree at Trevecca Nazarene University. Studying there allowed me to continue working at my regular job. The program was structured in a way that permitted me to work on my dissertation while I took classes. In 2015, three years after beginning, I completed my doctoral work.

Between the ages of thirty-seven and fifty-nine, the unthinkable happened in my life. A little boy from a broken home who lived on welfare and worked to buy the bare necessities of life was able to earn three college degrees. Of course, I never would have been able to begin working on any type of degree without my wife. I still could not financially afford an education. My wife worked at Trevecca so I could reach my goals. She never complained because she knew I was getting my education covered through the school's tuition remission program. Because of her sacrifice, I was able to pursue my bachelor's and master's degrees in church music and religion. No one accomplishes these things alone. It took me a long time to recognize and admit that. Without my wife of fifty years persisting in her work, I never would have been able to persist in my educational pursuits.

I have learned that growing up poor does not have to limit what you accomplish in life. The only thing that will hold you back is you. Make the choices today that will get you where you want to be tomorrow. The future is literally in your hands. You can create it one positive choice at a time.

MARVIN JONES *was born and raised in Virginia. He earned his BS, MA, and EdD degrees from Trevecca Nazarene University. He joined the Olivet faculty in 2017, where he serves as a professor in the School of Music. Marvin and his wife, Paula, are the parents of two adult children and have three grandchildren.*

MIDTERM SCARE IN THE RED ROOM
Lance Kilpatrick

The year was 1998. My first semester of college hit me like a freight train. I guess I'd always been what could be called an average student in high school. I wasn't a star athlete or an honors student. I was just me—an average guy trying to figure things out. Truth be told, the only thing I had really figured out was that I wanted to be a middle school teacher and, if I was lucky, maybe one day I could coach high school football. But when I stepped onto the campus of Olivet as a freshman, I had this nagging feeling that being average wasn't going to cut it anymore.

    I arrived on campus a couple weeks early to play college football. I was a walk-on athlete; there I was: below average already. I was plagued by negative thoughts. My assumption was that I could walk off just as easily as I had walked on, and no one would really care. I felt like a boy playing with men who were much stronger, much faster, and just better all around. They punished me for being weak and lacking confidence. One blessing from football was it gave me the time I needed to acclimate to campus life and get to know some other freshman guys on my floor before classes began.

The first few weeks of college were a whirlwind. I remember participating in the annual Ollies Follies, trying to find my way around campus, and attempting to make sense of all the new faces and places. My classes were a shock. The material was harder, the lectures faster, the assignments more demanding than anything I'd encountered before, and every test mattered. I was doing my best to keep up, but it felt like I was constantly one step behind.

Midterms arrived more quickly than I expected, and I was bracing myself for the inevitable. Back in those days, Olivet didn't have an online system that communicated every assignment or grade. We had to wait for periodic report cards to come in the mail. Back then, in the basement of Ludwig (or "Luddy," as we called it then) were rows of mini mailboxes that lined the walls, where students would stop to retrieve their mail. On that particular day, word was out that our midterm grades were in our mailboxes. So after dinner, I headed downstairs with four other guys so we could get our midterm grades.

I remember it vividly. We decided we would open our grades together down at a table in the Red Room (now named The Webb) and share the experience together. I had done my best to prepare—or so I thought. I'd taken notes, studied, and tried to participate in discussions. But when those midterm grades were released, it was like someone pulled the rug out from under me. Seeing those letters next to my courses made my stomach sink. My GPA was nothing short of disastrous. I felt a wave of panic and self-doubt crash over me. I looked across the table, and it looked like my buddies were experiencing a similar feeling. College was expensive. Was I throwing away my opportunity?

I wasn't alone. We all felt that same pang of desperation. We were at a crossroads. We were supportive of one another, but we each had to make our own decisions right then and there about our college lives. I could either let this define me, or I could take control of my situation. I wasn't one to give up easily, but this was different. College was unlike anything I'd faced before, and I realized I had to radically change my approach if I wanted to turn things around.

The next day, I decided I needed to transform my work habits and my mindset. First, I had to get organized. I bought a small whiteboard calendar and started mapping out my schedule in detail for the next month. I included everything: class times, study sessions, assignment deadlines, practice times, games, and anything else that came to mind. I realized I needed structure. The chaos of my previous approach was only making things worse.

Next, I tackled my study habits. I'd been relying on the same methods I used in high school, but clearly, they weren't sufficient. I wasn't successful doing college by myself. I needed the help of others. I started looking for others I could study with and who would help keep me accountable. I began to actively engage with my professors during class (and sometimes after class). It felt awkward at first, but it was worth it. They started to get to know me, and I started to get to know them. I can't tell you exactly how or why that helped, but somehow it did.

I began to embrace the challenge instead of shying away from it. I started to see each tough assignment as a chance to learn and improve, not just another hurdle to clear. I started to read. The effort I put in was starting to pay off—but only slightly. My grades didn't improve significantly in a week or even two weeks. The primary and immediate difference was that I felt a sense of accomplishment and self-efficacy that I hadn't felt before.

MIDTERM SCARE IN THE RED ROOM

Looking back, that midterm scare was a wakeup call that I desperately needed. When that first semester ended, I had earned two S's (passing), one B, one C+, two C's, and one D+. Yikes! That gave me a 2.12 GPA. Though that was a massive improvement from my midterm grades, I knew I couldn't become a middle school teacher with that record! Plus, the classes would only get harder (gulp). I knew even then that I wasn't given those grades; I had earned those grades. The experience forced me to reevaluate my habits and pushed me to develop new skills and strategies. College life wasn't going to be easy, but it was teaching me resilience and adaptability—lessons I carry with me to this very day. I couldn't afford to be an average student anymore. I was someone who had learned to work. I learned to face the challenges and the struggles. It wasn't an overnight miracle or a quick fix. It was slow and deliberate. And over time, I'm thrilled to announce today, the perseverance did pay off.

What about the other four guys in that group? Well, one of them didn't turn things around after that evening in the Red Room. He continued to do poorly in his classes and left Olivet at the end of the semester. I lost contact with him. I'm not sure where life took him. The other three proudly finished all four years at Olivet and earned their degrees. As for me, I finished all four years at Olivet and earned my teaching degree. And I never did walk off the football team. In fact, by my senior year, my teammates voted me to be one of our team captains; I was fortunate to start in every game that year! I eventually received my teaching license, began teaching at a middle school, and started coaching high school football. That initial midterm scare got my attention.

LANCE KILPATRICK *was raised in California. He earned a BA from Olivet and an EdD in curriculum and instruction from Liberty University. He joined the Olivet faculty in 2011 as an assistant professor of education and currently serves as the associate dean of the School of Education. Lance and his wife, Amy, are the parents of one son and two daughters.*

GRIEF AMIDST MILESTONES
Elyse Lamszus

In January one year, my husband, John, and I moved to Oak Park, Illinois, from suburban Glen Ellyn to be closer to downtown Chicago, where John worked. John would have preferred to move into the city, but my experiences of growing up on a farm with vast expanses of fields as far as the eye could see were still too fresh. Suburban living was a big-enough adjustment as it was, so we settled on Oak Park, a community just outside the city limits of Chicago, where a couple of dear friends were already living and the L could give John a much easier commute to work. We found a great condo downtown within walking distance of our new church, the Green Line, and all the shops and restaurants we could ask for. We loved our new community and looked forward to our future there.

At the time we moved to Oak Park, I was beginning my last semester of grad school at Northern Illinois University and looking for a full-time teaching job for the fall. We wanted to stay in the Chicago area for a variety of reasons, so my options were limited. I prayed earnestly that the five years I had spent in grad school would lead to something meaningful. And, though my dissertation wasn't completed yet, I prayed that fact wouldn't automatically disqualify me from consideration for a job. Although I was disqualified from most schools to which I applied for that very reason, in February I got an offer from Olivet, my top choice despite its considerable distance from Oak Park. I readily accepted. I never could have imagined this for myself as a kid growing up on a farm in rural Ontario. All my hard work seemed to be paying off, and I looked forward to the future of being an actual professor.

Spring turned to summer, and my attention turned full time to my dissertation. I wanted to write as much as possible before the demands of my first real job were upon me and the dissertation would have to take a back seat. I did take a delightful break in July to be with my family when my younger brother, Danny, and his wife, Corrine, welcomed a daughter, Aria, into the world. I loved being an aunt to my nieces on John's side of the family and was now excited to have this experience on my side of the family, too. The family had grown, and the gift of new life invigorated me with new hope for the future.

Summer turned to fall. I hadn't completed my dissertation yet, but it was time to start teaching at Olivet. I was fortunate to have had plenty of teaching experience in grad school, which prepared me as much as anything could have. However, the leap from 48 students in 2 classes to 136 students in 4 classes was overwhelming. There were many names to learn—students, faculty, staff, and administrators—as well as class sessions to plan, meetings to attend, and papers to grade. The workload was heavy. Still, I felt warmly welcomed and supported, and I quickly came to love the students. I felt affirmed that God had called me to this place for a purpose. I just didn't know yet that the purpose was as much for my benefit as it was for anyone else's benefit.

As I was getting ready to teach my literature students on October 6, 2014, I got a call from my mom. This was unusual because we primarily communicated over Facebook. So, rather than feeling excited to talk to Mom, I got a sinking feeling as soon as I saw her name on my caller ID. Sure enough, the call was bad news: Danny had cancer. I simply couldn't process the information. How could my twenty-six-year-old brother with a wife and almost three-month-old daughter have cancer? It made absolutely no sense. Sara, my department's administrative assistant, had a clear view from her desk to mine when my door was open, and she could see and hear that I had been rocked pretty badly by the news. Though I didn't yet know Sara all that well, she came and gave me a hug that strengthened me enough to head down the hall and teach my class. It sounds so cliché, but I truly felt like I was walking around in a bad dream: there I was, going through the motions of teaching my students, but it was all fuzzy and slow-motion and somehow not quite right. The future that had seemed so bright, so full of promise and purpose, was now cloudy and uncertain.

John and I had just started looking to buy a single-family home in Oak Park a week or two before we got news about Danny's diagnosis; we loved the condo we were renting but wanted to set down roots in the community and have more space for kids of our own in the next year or two. After the diagnosis, part of me wondered what right I had to dream about the future in such an optimistic way when my brother was undergoing cancer treatment. Part of me felt like the world should stop spinning, and we should all hold our breath until Danny was cancer free. Another part of me knew that wasn't possible—that I had to live, making the most of what God had given me because tomorrow wasn't promised. So we pressed forward into a whirlwind home search. It became a welcome distraction as we weighed the benefits and drawbacks of one property compared to another before we finally made an offer on a home we loved. The offer was accepted at the end of October, just in time for my birthday. It was a bright spot in a dark season for our family.

The dark season got darker. November 7 was a bright, crisp Friday, and the afternoon sunshine coupled with the prospect of the weekend ahead had me in a good mood. I even stopped by Starbucks for a chai latte to enjoy on my afternoon commute. Everything felt normal. But I was, for the moment, blissfully unaware of a new reality that would shatter all sense of normalcy. When I got home, I was surprised to see John there already, along with my friend Stephanie. They sat me down on the couch and told me the worst possible news: Danny had died. I can still feel the pain of that moment so viscerally. I couldn't breathe, couldn't see, couldn't hear. I couldn't process the information but felt like I was suffocating and drowning at the same time.

How could this happen? How would I survive the loss of my only brother and first friend? What about my family? How was I supposed to go back to work? How was I supposed to finish writing a dissertation? How was I supposed to move and set up a home and start a family?

It was simply too much. The grief was enormous, too much to bear alone. But praise God: I was not alone. I had family and friends walk through the darkness of that time with me. Coworkers, busy with their own classes, stepped in to cover mine while I was away. Students emailed me to let me know they were praying for me. And I clung to Isaiah 43:1–2:

> But now, this is what the LORD says—he who created you, Jacob, he who formed you, Israel: "Do not fear, for

I have redeemed you; I have summoned you by name; you are mine. When you pass through the waters, I will be with you; and when you pass through the rivers, they will not sweep over you. When you walk through the fire, you will not be burned; the flames will not set you ablaze."

I knew in my bones that these words weren't just for ancient Israel but were for me too. God was with me in my grief, and I wouldn't drown in it, even if it sometimes felt like I would.

To say that I persisted to finish the semester, move into our new house, complete the school year, defend my dissertation, and graduate with my PhD in 2015 doesn't feel quite right. I honestly don't know that *I persisted* so much as I leaned on family and friends, on my new church, and on my work community to carry me forward into a future that was darker without my brother yet not without grace and hope. That time was a blur of grief amidst the many milestones. My wider community made all the difference in shifting my focus from present pain and an unpromised future to God himself.

ELYSE LAMSZUS *was born and raised in Ontario, Canada. She earned a BA from Trinity Christian College and a PhD from Northern Illinois University. She has taught in the Department of English at Olivet since 2014. Elyse and her husband, John, reside in Oak Park, Illinois, with their two children.*

STARTING OVER, AGAIN
Stephen Lowe

Seven schools in thirteen years, counting kindergarten. Six of those schools were during the last nine years, including three different high schools. My family even moved the summer before my senior year, which turned out to be the most fitting way for me to finish my elementary and secondary education: graduating from a new high school in a new city and state.

While some people experience even more dislocation and separation than this during their school days, most do not. My wife had the stability of growing up in the same community throughout her school years. For those people raised in families who uproot and move regularly, many see it as an exciting adventure. My sister, who is a year younger than me, seemed to enjoy relocating, welcoming the chance to make new friends and experience different places. For me, though, it was a struggle. When I was young, my parents and teachers told me I suffered from homesickness, but it was more complicated than that—another kind of challenge in adjusting to new environments.

It is difficult to describe how upset I became inside whenever we moved, especially in my preteen years. We made our first move just as I finished the third grade, leaving Michigan for Minnesota. I can still clearly recall the last day of our first summer in the Twin Cities. It was Labor Day, and the new school year began the next morning. Not having any idea what was in store for me, I was excited that evening, anticipating the start of school and the chance to make some friends. I imagined it would be just like the school I had left in Michigan.

But at eight o'clock the next morning, as I arrived at my new school, I immediately realized it was very different. And I did not like it. Among other things, it seemed so noisy, and I felt lost and all alone. It was as if everyone else had a friend, knew where to go, and knew what to do. I felt like I was on the outside looking in, watching everyone move and hearing their excited voices talking and laughing all around me, but I was strangely disconnected from it. It was scary. I remember just wanting to leave and go back to my old school and friends in Michigan. But, of course, I could not, and that made me feel trapped.

Eventually, as the days and weeks passed, I settled into my new surroundings, but it took a long time for me to feel comfortable as a fourth grader in Minnesota. All through that autumn, I struggled with fear and anxiety at school. In the evenings, I sometimes got upset just thinking about having to go back the next morning. It was like that until Christmas break. Then, as I also remember quite clearly, things improved when I returned to school in January. Suddenly, I felt better. There was something about leaving my new school for an extended time and then returning that made it feel healthier and more familiar. I became comfortable and began enjoying school and my new friends. I was only nine years old and did not have much choice in the matter, but I found a way to persist.

Three years later, we moved again. The same feelings of loneliness, distress, and fear returned. At the time, I had only a couple months left in the sixth grade. I was that much older and better able to manage my emotions, but it was still rough. Then came two years of middle school in the same community—but at a new building and with mostly new classmates, which meant more adjustment. I finished with three high schools in four years. It helped that, as I entered the ninth grade in Ohio, my parents decided it would be better for me to attend a small Christian school. I made friends more easily there. However, after I finished the year, we moved across the state, where I began attending what would be my favorite school of them all. I settled in there more quickly, liked my classmates, became involved in sports and the yearbook, and the next year as a junior, I even made the morning announcements for the whole school on the PA system. I was looking forward to graduating from that school when, one more time, we moved. But as a senior, I only needed to attend half days, so I worked in the afternoons and evenings, saving money to buy a car and go to college.

The next fall, I arrived at Olivet. Yet another new place with unfamiliar faces. Although I had acquired a lot of emotional grit by then, I still felt uncomfortable during my first semester. Again, I did not know anyone well, including my roommate. Old feelings bubbled up, just like those I had when starting the fourth grade on that Tuesday morning in Minnesota. The cafeteria in Ludwig seemed more crowded and noisier than it was. My brain told me that if I just disciplined my emotions and persisted, I would eventually feel at home in Ludwig, Burke, and Chapman Hall, but my heart and stomach pressured me to leave and go home.

To keep busy that fall, I studied more than ever, making all A's and B's. For the first time, I stretched myself academically. I also clearly remember reading my Bible regularly. My dad had suggested I read one of the Psalms each day because they contain themes of praise, thanksgiving, and hope. Doing so lifted my spirits and made me feel a little better. A few months later, it happened again, just like in the fourth grade. I left for Christmas break, and when I returned for the spring semester in January, everything felt improved and more familiar, almost like a new home—or at least a home away from home.

 I had no control—no choice—over the moves that our family made before I came to Olivet. But I did have control over my decision to attend Olivet and persist to graduation. In that first fall semester, I could have gone home. Most days, I wanted to do just that, and I might have, were it not for all the moving and painful adjustment I experienced as a child. Looking back, I realize those early challenges increased my odds of staying at Olivet. After finishing at Olivet, I started grad school at a large public university in Ohio. Again, I knew absolutely no one when I arrived. Yet, slowly, I became more comfortable. Five years later, I completed my doctoral degree and returned to Olivet to serve as a professor of American history. The choice to move and tackle the challenges of graduate school was, in many ways, my biggest obstacle of all. I am not sure I would have overcome it had I not attended six schools in nine years while growing up.

 Some people would say that our heavenly Father planned—or at least permitted—all that difficult adjustment, adversity, and pain in my childhood so that as an adult I would persist academically and professionally and be able to share my story with you. When I was younger, I tended to view it that way too. But as I have moved through life, experiencing more pain and difficulty, I find myself spending less time trying to make neat, clean sense out of why I had to leave my friends and move so much when I was growing up and more time thinking about the promise of Romans 8:28: "And we know that in all things God works for the good of those who love him, who have been called according to his purpose." Our Father in heaven loves us, and he will mysteriously and unexpectedly redeem the inevitable pain and difficulty in our lives. I know that to be true because he has done so in mine.

STEPHEN LOWE *was born in Michigan. He also resided in Minnesota and Ohio for a season during his formative years. Stephen earned his BA from Olivet and his PhD in history from Ohio University. Since joining the Olivet faculty in 1993, he has taught American history, has served as department chair and dean of the College of Arts and Sciences, and currently serves as vice president for academic affairs. Stephen and his wife, Kim, have a son and a daughter.*

NAVIGATING THE UNEXPECTED
Heather McLaughlin

As I reflect on my life, several formative instances come to mind of when I wanted to give up and *did*. I quit piano as a tween because I hated practicing. I regret that now. I withdrew from an AP history test as a high schooler because I hadn't studied. I probably could have passed. However, I can also think of numerous instances when I wanted to give up and *didn't*. Here are two of those stories, both of which required me to navigate the unexpected.

The Snowy Drive

I grew up in Colorado Springs and loved going into the mountains. I'll never forget the first time I drove through them by myself. It was January 25, 1996. I was seventeen and had been invited to attend a Nazarene Youth Council meeting at Golden Bell Camp and Conference Center in Divide, Colorado, a forty-five-minute drive via Ute Pass. It was my first solo drive; I was excited. Admittedly, I was also concerned because the sun was setting, and the forecast called for snow. This was before we had cell phones with weather apps and GPS. Nonetheless, I decided I'd try to make it.

The first half of the trip was easy, but as I ascended higher into the mountains, the snow started falling. The flakes were fluffy and concentrated and soon began sticking to the road and accumulating.

When I arrived at the intersection where I was to turn off the main highway, the road was covered with five to six inches of snow with only a few slushy ruts barely visible. Nothing had been plowed. I found myself inching forward ever so slowly, not even going five miles per hour. It was a whiteout. I was terrified! Even though I was surrounded by pine and aspen trees, I could barely make out the road's edges, which were lined by deep ditches.

I tried turning on my high beams in hopes of better seeing the road ahead. That only made it worse, so I switched them back off. The panic of helplessness came over me. I was unsure what to do. Should I just stop? Should I pull over, wait, and wave someone down? Should I roll on at this snail's pace even though it would take hours and someone might crash into me? I was desperate. I remember praying, "God, help me. Please help me."

Then it occurred to me that maybe I could turn off the lights completely, but that didn't seem right. Or what about the parking lights? Might those work? I rotated the switch one notch, which dimmed the headlamps and produced a soft orange glow. The parking lights successfully illuminated the entire area around the car, probably ten to fifteen feet ahead. It was just enough that I could make out the curvature of the road, whether it veered to the right or to the left or slightly downhill. It was perfect. I felt a sense of relief. It was still a challenge, but the combination of the lamp's glow and the reflection of the fallen snow guided me safely to my destination. I arrived exhausted, with cramped fingers and an aching back. I'd been clenching and peering over the steering wheel for an hour straight, but I had made it. I didn't give up.

The experience reminded me of Psalm 119:105: "Your word is a lamp for my feet, a light on my path." When I unexpectedly find myself stuck in the snowstorms of life and lacking direction, I know God will provide his light and help me persist.

The Significant Exam

In the fall of 2011, I was a PhD student at the University of Kansas in the Department of Communication Studies. I'd finished my coursework, and the next hurdle was a written comprehensive exam. It was a partly sunny day when I pulled into a parking spot in the five-story garage at the Kansas Union and turned the engine off. I took a deep breath. This was it, the day I'd been anticipating. I pulled out a plastic card file box, popped open the lid, and saw my thick stack of 3x5 cards. Each card had handwritten citations, concepts, phrases, and statements. All were numbered and color coded with neon yellow, green, and pink highlighter markings. For six weeks I had been preparing for this day. I had created a comprehensive bibliography of my knowledge in four areas: communication theory, research methodology, and my two specialties: interpersonal communication and new technology. I'd annotated more than 298 articles.

I flipped through the Theory category of cards as a quick refresher, then put them aside, leaving them on the front seat. I headed toward the building where I was to take the exam. This was the first day of four. I was terribly nervous, even nauseated. I consciously took deep breaths as I walked, and whispered rhythmically, "Lord, give me strength. Lord, give me strength." I'd scouted out the exam room the day before.

It wasn't much bigger than a closet with bare white walls, one small vintage table, a simple chair, a computer monitor, a keyboard, and a mouse.

I greeted the proctor of the exam, signed in, and received a No. 10 envelope containing the questions, which were written by a committee of my professors, including my advisor. I was allowed to have blank sheets of paper and a pen, but that was it. No notecards. I had three hours to answer three questions about communication theory, and I anticipated typing three to four pages, double spaced with citations, for each. I powered up the monitor and opened a blank Word document. The cursor blinked at me. I prayed a quick prayer—"Lord, help me"—and opened the envelope. I unfolded the paper inside, revealing the three—wait, four? *Four* questions?

Panic set in. *Did I misunderstand the instructions?* Flustered, I realized this would give me less time to complete each question. I froze. Could I possibly write thoroughly and adequately, given this unanticipated extra question? What was going on? As a perfectionist and planner, this surprise overwhelmed me.

"Lord, help me!" I whispered fervently. I sat for another minute or so, motionless. Then I realized I hadn't even read the questions. I blinked until the words came into focus and read the first one. *Okay, that's not too bad,* I thought. I read the second. *This one is manageable,* I thought. The third was a little intimidating but, hopefully, doable. The fourth question was daunting and somewhat vague. I wasn't sure what I'd do. I wanted to give up, but I didn't.

I felt confident as I answered the first two questions. I scribbled an outline and concepts on the blank paper to map out my thoughts and then clacked the keyboard. Question one, done. Question two, done. Question three, almost done. I glanced at the clock and realized there wasn't much time left. I hastily finished the third question and typed about half a page of nonsense before the proctor came to get me. I hadn't really finished. I didn't have time to reread and proof my answers. I felt defeated. I wanted to cry. In fact, I did cry most of the way home. *I'm not going to pass*, I thought. *That was not fair!*

I called my parents and told them what happened, sobbing. "Forget this!" I announced. "It's not worth it!" I declared. "I'm done. I just want to quit."

As soon as those words came out of my mouth, it felt good. I felt a sense of freedom, realizing I *could* quit—if I wanted to. But did I really want to? I honestly can't remember if my parents said something, or if the process of venting allowed me to compose myself and return to logic. Probably both. No, I *didn't* want to quit. I had been through three years of a rigorous program, and it would be senseless to give up now.

An hour passed, and I settled down. I decided to email my advisor, bravely asking for clarification on the instructions, explaining my confusion and the circumstance. To my surprise, she responded almost immediately with a profuse apology, realizing the committee's mistake. She confirmed that indeed I was only supposed to answer three questions covering theory. A sense of relief flooded through me, and I cried again with a new emotion. I released the day's perceived failure and approached the next three days with a renewed confidence.

I'm so glad I didn't give up. The committee recognized the mistake and confusion of that first day. And, with the Lord's help, I passed all my written exams that week.

Both these experiences remind me that, whenever I find myself facing the unplanned and unfair surprises of life, the Lord will provide his strength and help me persist—whether mile by mile or question by question. Navigating the unexpected is his specialty.

HEATHER (ATTIG) MCLAUGHLIN *was born and raised in Colorado Springs, Colorado. She earned her BA from MidAmerica Nazarene University and her PhD in communication studies from the University of Kansas. She joined Olivet's faculty in 2014, teaching courses in multimedia production, speech, and public relations, and she serves as chair of the Department of Communication. Heather and her husband, Corey, adore their seven-pound Havanese dog, Candi.*

HURDLES IN TRACKTOWN
Kent Olney

The city of Eugene, home to the University of Oregon (U of O), is known as "TrackTown USA." The university's Hayward Field has hosted multiple NCAA track and field championships since the 1960s, and eight U.S. Olympic team trials have been held there since 1972—including every trial since 2008. I spent several years there as a young man. While I never participated in the university's legendary track program, I assure you I did jump many hurdles that landed me at fabled Hayward Field. Let me explain what I mean.

I was a married father of two sons, serving on the faculty of a state university where I taught sign language and interpreting courses. After completing the graduate application process at the U of O, including taking the GRE, I submitted my paperwork and patiently awaited word on my status. Having been on the dean's list during most of my undergraduate education, having earned two master's degrees from other schools, and having taught at a sister institution in the state, I assumed my chances of acceptance at the University of Oregon were good.

When the letter came in late March, however, it brought disappointment. Among 104 applicants, I was ranked sixteenth, but my heart sank when I read these words: "We have limited the incoming class to eight students." Not wanting to give up on my dream, I made an appointment with the graduate program coordinator. My intent was not to contest the decision but to determine how I might improve my chances if I decided to apply again the following year. The meeting was brief, cordial, and a bit awkward. When I asked the graduate director for advice on improvement, he assured me I was competitive in every area the committee evaluated. Then, perhaps to get me out of his office, he divulged that I was "second on the list of white males." My problem was not a qualifications issue but a demographics issue. Affirmative Action policies were in place that sought to recruit minorities and women at the U of O, and I did not fit the desired profile.

After taking some time to prayerfully consider next steps, I decided to reapply the following year. When the much-anticipated letter came the second time, I discovered the good news that the sociology program was expanding its admission to ten students, and I had moved up five places on the list. Heartened as I was, that still left me ranked eleventh and without a spot. I was on the outside looking in, the recipient of two consecutive rejection letters. Months passed. Finally, shortly before fall semester began, I received a phone call from the university informing me that one of the ten candidates ahead of me had withdrawn. The vacant position was offered to me. Although my ego was bruised, I accepted the offer and began my graduate studies in sociology. The initial hurdle had been tougher than expected, but I was on my way.

My first graduate course at Oregon was Classical Marxism. We were assigned twelve books to read—all written by or about Karl Marx. The demands were heavy, and I did my best to balance being a husband, father, and faculty member with being a full-time graduate student. I read all twelve books, wrote a long paper on Marx, drove seventy miles one way to attend every class session, and passed the course.

Courses on research methods and statistics followed. The detail demanded in those courses challenged me, but I excelled—until I earned a D on the final exam in an advanced statistics course. I was both surprised and embarrassed. I headed into that final exam with an A in the course, and I remember walking out of the exam room thinking I had done well. It was a sobering experience, to say the least, but I did pass the class. In another course, consisting of a handful of students and a professor gathered around a large seminar table, a female classmate disagreed with a comment I made one day and publicly expressed her view that I could not be trusted because I was a "white, heterosexual, patriarchal male."

Hurdles appeared everywhere, in different forms, often unexpectedly. The biggest hurdles, however, were yet to come. After completing all my coursework, it was time to take two comprehensive exams to exhibit mastery of specific content areas. The first exam covered the sociology of religion, culminating in an oral exam on multiple books and themes relevant to the subject. I sat in a room before three professors who, between them, held PhDs from Harvard, the University of Chicago, and the U of O. For an hour, I was grilled with one question after another. Things were going relatively well until near the end of the hour. When I attempted to explain the theme and conclusions of one final book, the Harvard-educated professor leaned forward across the table, pointed his finger in my face, and shouted, "You're wrong!" The exam came to an abrupt end. I had failed. I left and drove the seventy miles home in humility. My humiliation only increased when I arrived and discovered that my wife had planned a small party—with cake and streamers—to celebrate the anticipated milestone. The celebration dissolved into tears.

As only God could orchestrate, that same afternoon I received a personal letter in the mail from a missionary friend in Colombia, South America, who had heard of my graduate work and wrote to encourage me in my pursuit. The handwritten note urged me to "keep knocking" on the door of opportunity because the world needs more "godly professors." That letter and its timely message bolstered my courage. A few days later, I called the sociology department and asked if I might retake the comprehensive exam. Permission was granted. I reviewed the book that had made me stumble earlier and knew it from cover to cover when I returned for round two. I passed the exam. Jumping hurdles, I realized, often took multiple attempts. More than once, I was tempted to withdraw and quit the race. I am glad I kept going.

A few months later, my family and I moved across the country, and I joined Olivet's faculty. I had completed all the requirements for my PhD except for the dissertation. I secretly wondered if I could do it. Could I make it to the finish line? How would I find the time? Where would I get needed primary sources for my research project? While the details are too numerous to explain here, God helped me over those hurdles as well. Early mornings, Saturdays, and summers provided the time to focus on the project before me.

As a researcher, I hit a proverbial gold mine when I discovered that most of the materials I needed to complete my historical sociological study were contained in the attic of a private home in Wheaton, Illinois. I was studying the role that the Chicago Mission for the Deaf played in the formation of the early American deaf community, and the woman who possessed the relevant materials—personal letters, journals, church records, pictures, and more—lived just over an hour away from Olivet. She was the granddaughter of the man who founded the Chicago Mission for the Deaf in the late nineteenth century. Surprisingly, she not only granted me access to the historical documents but actually allowed me to load her grandfather's boxes into my car and take them to my office. Thus, I had what I needed to write what eventually became a 478-page dissertation over the next three years. It was the final hurdle in the eight-year marathon that culminated in earning my doctorate.

When I returned to the U of O for commencement, I lined up with the other graduates. A beautiful blue June sky made the surrounding Cascade Mountains more breathtaking than usual. Together, we graduates circled the track at Hayward Field before taking our place in the stadium. It was a symbolic victory lap. My family cheered from the stands as I stepped forward to receive my diploma; it felt like Olympic gold that day. The memory of multiple hurdles and the grueling marathon began to fade as we celebrated and enjoyed the closing ceremony. The hard work, failures, disappointments, and ultimate triumph combined to open new doors of opportunity that would have been impossible to experience any other way.

KENT OLNEY *was born and raised in Michigan. He earned a BA from Asbury College and a PhD in sociology from the University of Oregon. He joined the Olivet faculty in 1995, teaching sociology and serving as a department chair before accepting his current role as dean of the College of Arts and Sciences. Kent and his wife, Beth, have two sons and five grandchildren.*

WOODEN HANGERS
Beth Patrick-Trippel

Every fall, when thousands of families drop off their children at Olivet, I'm struck by two related thoughts. First, I realize these parents are giving an incredible gift to their kids. It will take a lifetime for these students to fully realize all the gifts their families have given them to make this journey possible. Of course, we often think of the financial sacrifices, but there are also gifts of time, energy, prayer, and encouragement that are just as valuable. These non-monetary gifts are so powerful that they may be what students will ultimately remember the most.

Second, I wonder how many of these same students will find a way to make it all the way to their graduation. How many will hang in there through the challenges that inevitably come? I've been a professor long enough to know that far too many students drop out and never reach their goal. There are so many pressures on students, and some of them get derailed by their challenges, but I'm always profoundly saddened when that happens. Looking back, that could have easily been my story.

Not every family is able to help their children financially. That certainly was the case for my family. I was a seventeen-year-old freshman whose parents couldn't even afford the gas money to take me to college, much less the tuition payments. My high school boyfriend dropped me off in a town thirty-five miles away so I could catch a ride with another family. Packed into his 1968 Camaro with a Bondo-colored paint job were all the things I thought I'd need for college.

The decisions of what to pack were not easy when college was a thousand miles away and I knew I wouldn't return until Christmas break. But two things I packed were gifts that I didn't fully appreciate until many years later. They weren't wrapped, and they weren't expensive. In fact, they were perhaps the only tangible gifts my parents could give me at the time: wooden hangers and an ironing board.

My family had struggled in poverty my entire life. We owned a family business that generally provided bare sustenance, but beyond that, we had nothing. When I packed for college, the clothes I brought were those I had purchased from working through high school. My parents couldn't send me with a check to pay tuition or even gas money for travel. But my mom wanted me to have *something*.

Mom had been saving S&H green stamps for years. (Yes, I know this tells my age because some of you will have to google "green stamps" to understand.) She went to the redemption store with all her books of green stamps and returned with a gift for me to take to college: a full-sized ironing board. In the 1980s, all our clothes were ironed and starched and pristine. Perhaps some might not appreciate an ironing board as a gift today, but I loved it! At the time, I didn't think much about her sacrifice. Now, I know she could have instead bought something that would have made her difficult life a bit easier.

How my mom came to give me most of her wooden hangers to take to college is a bit foggy. I'm sure she suggested it, but I'm not sure why I accepted them. The wooden hangers were possibly the only items she owned that would be considered high quality. I remember that she hated standard wire hangers—partly because they were flimsy but mostly because they made an indentation on any clothing hung on them. To her, wooden hangers were a sign of prosperity, and she wanted me to have them. So she exchanged the sturdy, wooden hangers in her closet for the wire, drooping hangers in mine.

Perhaps I shouldn't have accepted the gift. Certainly, that would have fit with my self-sufficient attitude. But what a disservice that would have been, both to my mother and myself! Not only would I have deprived her of the ability to give gifts to her children, but I also would have deprived myself of an opportunity for gratitude.

I arrived at college that fall to learn many, many lessons—some I didn't even realize I'd learned until days, months, or even years later. I was the only girl on my floor with a full-sized ironing board, so everyone shared it. For my entire four years of college, it sat in the hall for everyone to use.

And as I looked at those wooden hangers every day, I was reminded of my mom and her sacrifices. I looked at them all the more when my mom was diagnosed with pancreatic cancer. Those were hard and painful days. There were times when my sister and I made the two-thousand-mile round trip twice a month. It would have been much easier to stay home for a semester. But my mom wouldn't even let us entertain the idea of quitting. So we traveled back and forth as often as possible, and God protected us across those many miles. Those hangers in my closet were a reminder that my mom had given what little she could. How could I do any less? With God's help and the help of my professors, friends, and home church, both my sister and I made it through to graduation.

My mom wasn't at our graduation, at least not in a physical sense, but as I packed up my dorm room, she was there. And she was there when my ironing board made it to a new apartment near grad school, then on to my first job as a professor.

Over the years, I've watched students follow a similar path. I've known students who entered college with their own equivalent of wooden hangers to motivate them. They faced difficult decisions, broken engagements, and every other type of challenge. Yet they persisted and made it to their goal. They are my heroes.

As I look in my closet today, all these years after college, I still see some of those same hangers that were given to me so many years ago. I've added many, many wooden hangers to them over the years, but I still have a deep gratitude for the originals. While I've gone on to lead a blessed life, those hangers continue to remind me of my roots and the perseverance it took to get where I am today. I pray for my current students—that they will stay the course when life is hard and when hope rests on no more than hangers in a closet.

BETH PATRICK-TRIPPEL *was born and raised in Florida. She holds a BA from Trevecca Nazarene University and an EdD from Nova Southeastern University. An Olivet faculty member since 1994, she serves as a professor of communication in the College of Arts and Sciences. Beth is married to Kevin, and they live in Kankakee, Illinois.*

23
WHY ME?
Charles Perabeau

"Why me, Lord? Why me?"

It was 2:15 a.m., and this time I didn't have a ride. My car, one of several beaters I owned during my college years, was in disrepair—again. My usual backup plan was to borrow my roommate's green Buick station wagon from the 1980s, affectionately known as the Pickle. However, Ed was away, and that triggered the option of last resort: walking to work. My shift at the Eagle Foods grocery store started at 3:00 a.m. and calling off was out of the question, for I needed every dollar I could earn. So I bundled up, briefly rousing the RA sleeping in front of the door separating the Chapman Hall lobby from the first-floor rooms, and quietly embarked on the 1.7-mile journey in the brutal cold in the middle of winter. Already feeling numb in my toes by the time I reached Stadium Drive, I crossed over from Bourbonnais into Bradley just past the football field. By the time I reached North Street past the high school with the railroad crossing in sight, tears flowed abundantly—a combination of the sheer cold, my building frustrations, and a sense of helplessness. I thought, *This just might be the final straw.*

"Why me, Lord? Why me?" I was certain that no one else in the entire Olivet student population was walking to work at this hour in early February. *Why can't my experience be more normal?* I thought. Jealousy of other students threatened to take root. But the current tuition bill needed to be paid in order for me to register for the next term's classes, so I placed one foot in front of the other in the stillness of the night (morning, more accurately) and trudged forward. *One semester at a time*, I told myself.

I had moved into Chapman well before most other freshmen. A few others arrived early for band, football, or other matters; I came for work. I had transferred my employment to the store from one I had begun working at a year earlier in my hometown of Galesburg, Illinois. I thought it would be good to have a head start working in a new environment before adding in classes. Even before the semester began, I was exhausted.

College life was new for both my family and me. Although my parents were supportive of my decision to attend Olivet, they didn't understand the college world. Neither of them finished high school, although my father received his GED as a part of his career in the Army. And while they had forged a home life of modest means for my siblings and me, they both had grown up knowing poverty firsthand. My father was one of eighteen children and often wore his mother's coat to school as a child because he lacked his own. As for my mother, she believed she was marrying up, not down, the social ladder. Together they saved well but lived frugally, and I assumed that paying for college was my responsibility without giving it a second thought. They had provided me with a warm, loving, and stable upbringing, and I hoped they would be proud of me as a college alumnus one day.

But now the struggle was real, and the rubber was meeting the road—literally—as I took another step forward toward

Eagle. This was one of those times—a make-it-or-break-it moment—that might determine not only whether I made it to work that day but also if I would persevere to graduation.

In the midst of tears, self-pity, doubt, and bone-chilling temperatures, an awareness—more than that, a revelation—fell fresh on me: God had called me. And there was no doubt that he had. I remembered the occasion from three years earlier so vividly just then. At the age of sixteen, I had gone across town to a revival service held at the smaller Nazarene church—the one that, a few years later, would permanently close. There weren't many people there that evening, maybe fifty or so. But God was there, and he caught me completely off guard as he spoke so clearly to me.

"*My desire is that your life be dedicated to full-time vocational ministry,*" he said. I didn't resist, nor was I displeased. Rather, it was more of a confirmation, a definitive declaration bringing clarity to ambiguous stirrings I had felt within. Now it was clearer to me than reality itself, and I immediately informed my pastor when I next saw him.

I knew the call to ministry included academic preparation; I dared not take the responsibility to represent God lightly. This necessitated attending college in addition to continuing to nurture my relationship with God and his people. Yes, college would be expensive, but I would avail myself of the wisdom, resources, and mentorship of seasoned clergy and faculty who had spent decades walking with the Lord and reflecting upon Scripture, theology, and practical ministry. The tears began to yield to an emerging smile as I knew God was with me once again. He had called me, and knowing that was enough to sustain me. "The one who calls you is faithful, and he will do it" (1 Thessalonians 5:24).

There would be other moments, even seasons, when the way forward was challenging. During the fall of my senior year, I worked three jobs—at Eagle, at the university's radio station (WONU), and as a teaching assistant for Spanish—and only had five overnights off the entire semester. Later in ministry, there would be challenges for which I felt ill equipped, lonely, and inadequate. Like others, I haven't escaped the loss of my parents, and I've faced potentially derailing crises.

My older self would advise my younger self differently. My sleeping varied in length and occurred at random hours. I missed out on lots of social engagements at school. Student loans, when handled responsibly, are a valid source of financial aid and helped me pay my school bills. Somehow, by the grace of God, I persevered and acquired a grit that would benefit me in later years as I leaned into and stood upon my calling.

The revelation I received back then still falls fresh today: he has called me. He has led me in ways I couldn't have imagined since that forty-minute walk on a freezing winter morning when the Pickle was unavailable. I later graduated not only from Olivet but also from Loyola University and Drew University. I married the love of my life, who has nurtured and supported my calling, and God has blessed us with three remarkable sons. The privilege of serving an urban, multicultural Nazarene congregation as pastor for more than a decade brought pure joy, deep relationships, and blessings to our entire family. And I still shake my head in disbelief that the Lord has been so kind as to allow me to fulfill my calling now as the dean of the School of Theology and Christian Ministry following seventeen years of teaching sociology at Olivet.

I confess that all these experiences still cause me to ask, "Why me, Lord? Why me?" However, my perspective has changed. Rather than asking out of frustration and self-pity, the question now comes from a heart of wonder, humility, and gratitude. As I look back over the years, I realize it has been the grace of God that has sustained and carried me along the way. His calling provided the bedrock for me at every moment of insecurity, doubt, and exhaustion, and it has proven sturdy and stable. These markers in my journey with God, and many others like them, confirm that "he who began a good work" in me will see it through to completion (Philippians 1:6). I've found that to be true even on frigid mornings when I'm stuck without a Pickle.

CHARLES PERABEAU *was born in Germany and grew up in Galesburg, Illinois. He earned his bachelor's degree from Olivet and his PhD in sociology and religion from Drew University. Since joining the Olivet faculty in 2005, he has taught both undergraduate and graduate students. In 2022, after serving in the Department of Behavioral Sciences for nearly two decades, he became the dean of the School of Theology and Christian Ministry. He and his wife, Gayle, have three adult sons.*

TOGETHER AS ONE
Amber Residori

When I was ten years old, my twin sister, Michelle, my older sister, Sonya, and I got off the school bus, walked into the house, and found our mother crying. It was obvious she had been crying a long time. Her eyes were swollen and red, and tears kept falling even as she tried to reassure us. Crying like this wasn't common in our family, so naturally we were concerned. We tried a few times to get her to tell us what was wrong, but she just shook her head—she didn't have words. Eventually, she gathered herself enough to ask us to go outside and play until our father came home from work. She said we'd talk once Dad was there.

Several hours later, Dad pulled into the driveway. We gave them a few minutes and then stuck our heads in the door to see if we could come in. We noticed that Dad was now also crying. Mom's tears and the permission to play before homework were strange enough, but seeing Dad crying really increased our worry. They sent us outside again to play, telling us they would call us in when they were ready to talk.

When Dad finally called us in, it was dark outside. We abandoned our game of night tag and headed to the kitchen table for a family meeting. It took a while for him to gain his composure, but he finally explained that the medical tests recently conducted with my sister Michelle revealed she had cancer.

As ten- and thirteen-year-old girls who were busy with things like night tag, we had no idea what it meant to have cancer. Dad explained that we would be driving Michelle and Mom to Indianapolis, which was four hours away, during the upcoming weekend. The two of them would live there temporarily, work with a team of doctors, and begin a long series of treatments to hopefully kill the cancer.

As he talked, we slowly began to understand the magnitude of what he was describing. We also noticed that he hadn't described how and when this battle with cancer would all end. Dad finished his careful description of what we were facing and asked if we had any questions.

I'll never forget his response when Michelle looked him in the eye and asked, "Daddy, will I die?"

Dad had several choices in that moment: protect her from the truth, beat around the bush, or even lie. With love in his eyes, he said, "You might, honey, you might. Cancer is that serious. But I can tell you, Michelle, that I will never lie to you about this journey. I will be honest, probably to a fault, because, whatever is ahead, I want you to never worry or be afraid that it's worse than you know. We will be beside you, and we will walk through this together with transparency and with love."

Then he turned to Sonya and me and said, "I want you to know that this just became the number-one priority of our family. As one—as *one* family—we will come together, sacrifice, tap into every resource available, and move mountains to ensure that Michelle gets the best medical treatment. We will trust God and his plan in this situation, but from this moment forward we will work together as one family. There will likely be unkept promises, compromises, responsibilities, and jobs you don't like or aren't used to doing, but as one family we will walk this road together."

Michelle and my mom spent about four months in Indianapolis battling cancer. Sonya, Dad, and I would leave school on Friday afternoons, drive to Indy, stay with Mom and Michelle all weekend, and then be back on Monday morning just in time to get on the school bus for another week of school. Dad worked two jobs to pay the extra medical bills. Sonya was responsible for ensuring we ate breakfast, had lunches packed, did our homework, and were on the bus for school each day. Everybody had new chores, and it was all hands on deck.

Over the months, Michelle looked worse and worse when we visited, and all the other children on her medical floor slowly passed away. We learned at a young age that cancer was ruthless, and we prayed diligently that Michelle would survive and come home. Gradually, she started looking more like herself. She was in remission. She was weak. She had many follow-up visits and trips to Indy, as well as medical complications over the next seven years. But she was alive, she was home, and she survived.

Eventually, she even thrived. In fact, her son and my daughters now attend Olivet together! We thank Jesus for such mercy and answered prayers!

During all those years, there was often talk about me going to college someday. No one in my family had ever earned a college degree. While I loved the idea, I didn't fully know what it meant. We had never filled out financial aid paperwork, heard of a Stafford Loan or Pell Grant, or visited a college campus. Frankly, college was as foreign to my family as cancer had once been. We had no idea where to even begin.

My high school counselor gave me a scholarship application and explained that I should fill it out if I wanted to attend college. I filled out the form by myself and, as an afterthought, wrote on the very bottom the following sentence: "Due to my twin sister's extensive battle with cancer, my parents were unable to set aside financial resources for me to attend college."

God answered prayers again and, to my shock, I received twelve scholarships. I was amazed. Though I was a solid student, I knew there were more deserving kids. Yet my community had surrounded me and set into motion an opportunity that changed the trajectory of my life.

Under my mom's watchful eye, I wrote personalized thank-you notes to each of the twelve individuals and organizations who provided a scholarship. Those gifts made college a reality for me and got me started on my educational journey. By my sophomore year, I was not only attending Olivet full time, but I was also working full time at Boz Hot Dogs. By my junior year, I was a full-time college student and was working full time at Boz and full time at Riverside Medical Center.

I graduated in four years with my degree in psychology and moved immediately into my career. I stayed in the area and put down roots. For twenty years, I worked with adolescents who struggled with severe emotional and behavioral disorders. I went on to complete my master's degree in social work administration from the University of Illinois and eventually landed right back at Riverside Medical Center, where I opened two inpatient psychiatric units for adolescents struggling with mental health crises.

In 2013 Olivet asked me to come back and teach in their Department of Social Work and Criminal Justice. I soon became the department chair. Two years later, I became the dean of the School of Life and Health Sciences. Along the way, I earned my doctoral degree in education with a focus on ethical leadership and became the first in my family to hold a doctorate. In 2020 I became the dean of the College of Professional Studies.

I'll be forever grateful to those twelve scholarship donors who invested in me many years ago. Their gifts are still multiplying. For students like me who are the first in their families to attend college and who have extra hurdles to climb: education is the path out of poverty. Your story is unfolding. When you get tired or hit obstacles, remember that you're fulfilling a calling on your life that is bigger than you. Move mountains to invest in yourself. Generously thank the people who support you. Give God the glory. And, when you graduate, grab hold of future generations and invest in their success.

At a young age, I learned the power of working together as one. I learned that nobody could fight cancer or finish college alone. The same is true today. As one individual, one group, one university, one community—*as one*—we invest in the lives of students, knowing full well that we can expect that investment to have a ripple effect that changes lives, shapes communities, and impacts the world.

AMBER RESIDORI *was born and raised in Indiana. A licensed clinical social worker, she earned a BA and EdD from Olivet and an MSW from the University of Illinois. Since joining the Olivet faculty in 2013, she has taught in the social work and RISE programs, served as chair of the Department of Social Work and Criminal Justice, served as dean of the School of Life and Health Sciences, and currently serves as dean of the College of Professional Studies. Amber and her husband, Jeff, have two daughters.*

25
NAOMI JOY'S FOOTPRINTS
Jeffrey Rice

I think about her often. Each time, a million questions race through my mind. Some are the same, and some are different. Some make me smile, and some make me sad.

What's she doing?
Who are her friends?
What's she like?
What's her favorite color?
What's her favorite food?
What is she studying?

In my mind's eye, I'm sitting with her, talking, laughing, and enjoying a cup of coffee (if she is like me) or a cup of herbal tea (if she is like her mama). I've imagined her playing games with her sisters or helping them with schoolwork. As these questions and thoughts flood my mind, I know they will remain unanswered. I'll never see her smile. I'll never hear her laugh. I'll never know her friends. Parents aren't supposed to outlive their children.

As I sit in the college cafeteria, I'm surrounded by a thousand students. They are the same age as she would have been. I am, either by innate character or observational curiosity, a people watcher.

More questions flood my consciousness as I look at the faces of these college students.

I wonder whom she would be hanging out with.

I look at their clothes and hair.

I wonder what her style would be. Would she have long hair or short? Would she prefer dresses or jeans? Would she wear contacts or glasses?

I close my eyes, and for a brief moment reality is suspended as I listen to the laughter of those college friends and imagine her sitting with that friend group, creating memories that would last a lifetime. A *lifetime*. That's a strange word. It sounds like an eternity, but, for our daughter, her lifetime was only ten days.

My wife, Sheila, has the following reflections:

Naomi Joy made her surprising debut in the summer of 2005, four months too early. We stayed by her side day and night, as often as we were allowed. They call the Neonatal Intensive Care Unit (NICU) a "roller coaster ride," and it truly was. The doctors did everything they could do to save her and help her develop during those ten days. Despite feeling extreme despair and even depression at times, we felt God's peace amid the difficulty, knowing that God was with us every step of the way.

The first several months and years following were the most challenging for me because I was going through not only hormonal changes after a pregnancy but also postpartum depression and grief from Naomi Joy's death. I just kept clinging to Jesus. I kept holding on. I kept doing the next thing in life, working, taking care of our home, surviving. We continued to attend church, read our Bibles, pray, cry out to God, attend grief counseling, and live as best we could.

How does one get over such a loss? The truth is, you don't. You learn to live with it. You live one day at a time. To paraphrase part of a movie I enjoy: You wake up in the morning and remember to breathe. You keep doing that every day until you no longer have to remember. When you wake up, you just breathe.

Tragedy like this has the singular ability to shape you or destroy you. The choice is yours. You can choose the path that leads to destruction, or cling to Jesus and choose the path that will shape you and help you mature and grow. The journey toward healing, toward persisting, isn't easy, but it is possible. Grief becomes part of you—but just a part. It doesn't have to define you. There is hope—if you choose it.

Sheila again offers her perspective:

We wanted nothing more than to be parents. But since we were unable to conceive again, we considered adoption. It took some time for me to convince Jeffrey that adoption was our best option. Finally, he opened himself to the idea. We then attended a meeting that discussed various approaches to adoption. After careful prayer and deliberate conversation, we decided a domestic adoption was the most logical choice for us. We contacted an adoption agency, submitted the mounds of necessary paperwork, and went through adoption training.

The hardest part of the entire process was waiting. But we waited. Waited to hear from our case worker. Waited to be connected to a birth mom. Waited to have a home study completed. We waited from 2005 until 2010 to finally become parents, which felt like an eternity for young expectant parents. Looking back, we can see that God's hand was in all the waiting because he was doing something in his timing.

It can be difficult to see God working while in the depths of struggle. Despite faith, upbringing, or innate character, thoughts of hopelessness creep into a person's consciousness. Even though Sheila and I were surrounded by a crowd of believers praying with us constantly, feelings of hopelessness were ever present. But we also knew God was there. We clung to his Word.

I'm not sure who coined the phrase "hindsight is 20/20," but we found it to be true. Looking back over our journey, we see evidence that God was there every second of every day. His guiding hand and masterful direction orchestrated the impossible. Only a God who is all knowing, all seeing, and all powerful could have influenced the sequence of events that occurred.

Sheila explains some of what happened as we continued on during those days:

After many bumps along the way, God led a birth mom to our profile at a pregnancy resource center in another town. She wanted to meet us in person, and, after meeting us, she was sure we were the right parents for her baby. We met her when she was three months pregnant and maintained visits with her to hear the baby's heartbeat and see the sonogram. She even invited me to be present during our baby's birth! However, our journey to becoming her parents was a bumpy ride. We feared the birth mother might back out. Then we ran into some trouble with the hospital nurses. But God intervened, and we were eventually able to bring the precious little girl home.

Four years later, through a loose connection with friends who had also adopted, we were connected to another birth mother seeking adoptive parents for her newborn daughter. So, after many months and many trials, in a distant state, another child was added to our family. There are many more details about each of their adoption stories. God was in every single one of those details.

Through all these experiences we have discovered that, as we go through life in our fallen world, human struggle is commonplace. Tragedies happen, and we often go through hardships that seem impossible to endure. Sometimes the hardships are so overwhelming that you feel you are going to break. I encourage you, dear reader, to persist. Cling to God. Trust in him even in the times when he feels so very far away. He is there—an invisible companion to love, care, and carry us through even if his presence isn't tangible.

During our deepest distress, Sheila and I found ourselves clinging to the following verse from Isaiah. It remains on our refrigerator today, a reminder of God's faithfulness: "I will go before you and will level the mountains; I will break down gates of bronze and cut through bars of iron. I will give you hidden treasures, riches stored in secret places, so that you may know that I am the LORD, the God of Israel, who summons you by name" (45:2–3).

As Sheila and I look back on our journey of loss and hope, of hurt and healing, of desperate sorrow and jubilation, we see God's hand. It was a journey we never chose, one that began with the devastating death of our precious ten-day-old baby girl. The darkness of that hour has given way to joy as we hear the laughter and see the smiles on our other daughters' faces. While Naomi Joy's footprints left a mark that will never be erased, the story of her loss didn't define us. God's faithfulness has the last word.

JEFFREY RICE spent his earliest years in Canada before moving to Illinois. He earned his BA from Olivet and his doctorate in computer science from Colorado Technical University. He began his Olivet employment in 2001 and joined the faculty in 2018. He teaches courses in computer science and cybersecurity, and he directs the computer science program. Jeffrey and his wife, Sheila, have two daughters on earth and one in heaven.

26
TEARS OF PERSISTENCE
Beth Schurman

There I was again, sitting at our kitchen table at one in the morning, working on my dissertation. I was used to being tired and stressed with working full time, completing a PhD program, and having three young children, so when the usual nagging thoughts of *just go to bed* set in, I pushed them back like I always did. Usually that worked, so I didn't expect the tears that came pouring down my cheeks seconds later. I was crying. No. I was sobbing.

This wasn't the first time I had cried from overworking myself. As a state swimmer in high school, I remember hot tears filling my goggles when I dragged my physically and mentally exhausted body out of the water after not placing as well as I had hoped. The tears also came at times during my undergrad and MA programs for some of the same reasons—I had taken on too much, my expectations were too high, and I had worked myself to the point of exhaustion. You get the picture.

The thing is, for most of my life, persistence wasn't really something I thought much about. As someone who has always had a bit of a Type A personality, persistence felt like something I might have to do if I didn't plan well enough or work hard enough—patterns I tried to avoid at all costs. And, honestly, living that way worked for a really long time. It didn't matter how much time, energy, or sleep I had to sacrifice. I would Get. It. Done. (That phrase literally adorns a sign in my office.) Work harder, faster, better, and everything will be fine. And I did.

But this time was different. The tears were heavier. In the past, I was always able to shrug them off and remind myself, "I can do this," or, "It's not that big of a deal." But these tears didn't just run down my cheeks; they bore into my soul. They came with a painful realization I couldn't avoid. My mind drifted away from the task at hand and my goals for that evening (goals I had written on our refrigerator each week to encourage my husband and even our kids to hold me accountable!) to a more somber question: *Is this all worth it? Are the countless nights of little sleep, the numerous missed hours with family and friends, and the constant mental and physical strain really worth it?*

I know most of you—when you are facing the clock at 2:00, 3:00, or even 4:00 a.m.—know the feeling of that constant pressure to do more and be more, to excel at anything and everything, to take on *just one more* task or responsibility. It will all be okay, right?

That is the interesting thing I have come to learn about persisting. For many of us, it's not a matter of overcoming that one big obstacle or event in our lives but a nagging, constant, sometimes painful way of life. The recurring questions haunt us. Is it good enough? Am *I* good enough? Then come the daily reminders of failure. For me, this is the email from my kids' teachers of forgotten items at home or the unintentional but stinging comments from one of my kids that store-bought cinnamon rolls are fine, but So-and-So's mom made homemade ones for the team. Although most of you may not have parent guilt (yet), you understand the struggle of balance and wellness, of being productive versus being present, and the cost of striving for perfection.

My tears that night taught me that living life like that has consequences. I don't mean to suggest that you shouldn't try your best or put your best work into the things you do, but I do mean to suggest there is value in struggle, and there is also value in simply existing. Prioritizing some things over other things always comes at a cost.

I used to believe that, if I wasn't working toward perfection, I was *just* persisting, and I've come to believe not only is that not true, but it's also not a healthy way to live. Maybe perfection and persistence don't need to have a dichotomous relationship because re-envisioning this relationship changes everything about how we live. What if persistence *was* our goal instead of it being what we do when we don't *meet* our goals? A verse I have often relied on to remind my overactive, over-analytical, anxious mind is Psalm 46:10, which reads in part, "Be still." I confess this isn't something that comes easily to me.

My tears were also a painful reminder that there are times when God calls us to persist. In my own life, it has meant I need to cut myself some slack when my CV isn't as long or impressive as my colleagues', or when I didn't quite meet my goals for the day or the year. Although most of you are only on the cusp of your professional careers, I think you know what I mean. In what areas of life do you need to stop working toward perfection and find simple joy in persisting? After all, we all make mistakes, we all fall short, and sometimes we need to stop trying so hard to be perfect and focus more on what we can learn from the moments when we're not.

That night served as a healthy reminder that I wasn't alone in my tears. Did you know Jesus cried? This is something else I've had to remind myself time and again when sitting in front of my computer literally in tears, feeling like I just can't do it, when I've lacked the time, energy, or mental capacity to keep going. The nights in the dorm room or at home when everyone else is sleeping and you know you're going to have to pull an all-nighter to get your paper or project done. John 11:35 tells us that even Jesus wept. It's okay to feel sad or disheartened when you face obstacles, big or small. It's what makes us human.

I'd be kidding you and myself if I told you I finally figured it all out after that late-night revelation more than ten years ago. I did get back to work that night, and I did finish my dissertation later that year, as planned. That night, however, has served as a reminder that there really isn't a right or wrong way to persist, and there is value in both the struggle and the process. Persistence isn't always crossing the finish line first but embracing the journey. It's knowing when and where to place our time and energy, and it's even knowing when it's time to step back or take a break. Whatever it is that you're working toward today, whether that is just getting through that next class or getting into that prestigious graduate program, I encourage you to keep stride. Remember that, through tears of joy or tears of pain, in moments when persistence feels like your best or your worst, God is with you always. He is there guiding your journey, protecting your path, weeping alongside you, and cheering you on.

BETH SCHURMAN is a native of Kankakee County, where she has lived her entire life. She completed a BA in English education at Olivet and a PhD in language and literacy from Purdue University. After teaching English at a local high school, she returned to Olivet and joined its faculty in 2006. She has served in the Department of English as a professor and now as department chair. Along with her department duties, Beth currently serves as the director of Olivet's Writing Center. She and her husband, Jeff, have four children.

THE CREATIVE PROCESS OF PERSISTENCE
Jon Seals

I grew up in rural Appalachia, where cultural resources were scarce. Yet I was driven by an intense longing to connect with a world I had only glimpsed through literature and film. From a young age, I determined to pursue a career in academia and the arts; art and education's power to transform lives and inspire change fascinated me. However, I faced financial challenges, self-doubt, and moments of discouragement that tested my resolve.

After completing my undergraduate degree at Olivet, I was accepted into two prestigious graduate programs. These were exciting opportunities, but they came with challenges. The academic workloads were demanding, and I struggled to balance my studies with the part-time jobs needed to support my family. I felt overwhelmed and unsure of my ability to succeed in such competitive environments.

During a particularly difficult season, I hit rock bottom. The pressure of coursework, combined with financial stress, left me feeling physically, emotionally, and spiritually defeated. It was a pivotal moment that forced me to confront my fears and reassess my goals. During this time, I was invited to create a painting live during several services in Marquand Chapel on the campus of Yale Divinity School.

Painting in front of my esteemed professors and classmates was a challenge I cautiously embraced. The invitation became more than just an opportunity to create a final product; it became a chance to showcase the painting process for everyone to experience. The entire process included stress, high expectations, and internal and external challenges. Through the experience, I felt a connection to the group I had not known before. Conversations and relationships developed that would not have been possible had I been painting alone in a sterile, isolated studio. Over time, I realized that the road to success would not be easy, but it was a journey worth taking with others.

In moments of doubt, I found strength in the support of my family, mentors, and peers. They reminded me that perseverance is not about avoiding failure but continuing to move forward amidst setbacks. With their encouragement, I learned to view challenges as opportunities for growth. I stopped fixating on some future finished product and began to celebrate and expose the process to which I was committed, with all its starts and stops and perceived and actual flaws. These latter elements provide access points to connect with others, let them in, and grow stronger together.

As a professor now, I am often asked to share my journey with students who are just beginning to navigate the complexities of professional life in the arts. I understand that the path to success is rarely straightforward, linear, or one-dimensional. Furthermore, much depends on one's definition of success. Life is full of obstacles, and my experiences have taught me that perseverance is the key to navigating adversity in whatever forms it is experienced, whether systemic or personal.

THE CREATIVE PROCESS OF PERSISTENCE

Difficulties often become opportunities for inspiration when making art. The creative process is inherently optimistic, characterized by continuous movement and activity amid countless challenges and unknowns. Each action leads to a response, inviting artists into a dialogue between their vision, materials, and outcomes. This dynamic nature of art mirrors life, where adversity can be transformed into fuel for growth and perseverance. Often, we mistake persistence as something possessed. Works of art are often viewed similarly, presented complete and polished to apparent perfection. Artists themselves are mistakenly seen as having a gift that arrives fully formed. I disagree on all counts. The most compelling works of art reveal the process, celebrate transitions of destruction and formation, and invite others to experience the creative act.

Interestingly, a frequently quoted Bible passage emphasizes process over product: "Consider it pure joy, my brothers and sisters, whenever you face trials of many kinds, because you know that the testing of your faith produces perseverance" (James 1:2–3). The twist, of course, is finding joy in times of trial, but there is also an indication that perseverance is something continual, not a singular achievement.

Perseverance is not an isolated event in times of trouble; it is an accumulation, or series, of small steps, choices, and decisions. It is a conviction built over time that forms patterns of perseverance. Success does not come from one giant step but from continual effort. Each attempt builds resilience, equipping one to handle future challenges. In painting and drawing, there is an Italian word, *pentimento*, from the verb *pentirsi*, meaning "to repent." It translates to "repentance" in English. The plural form is *pentimenti*. It refers to the presence of earlier drawn lines, shapes, forms, or painted strokes that have been altered and painted over. The works of artistic masters are often authenticated by the presence of *pentimenti*. These edits, attempts, stops, and starts often reveal the originality of the work. The presence of mistakes and the persistence to keep going demonstrate mastery.

Life is a journey filled with challenges that test our strength and resilience. Through these trials, we learn the true essence of perseverance. Persistence is a series of lived experiences, not something one simply reads about. However, allow me to illustrate what I mean with one more personal story.

In 2024 I faced a medical emergency that altered my perspective on life and perseverance. I experienced a condition known as *status epilepticus*, a series of prolonged seizures resulting in a complete loss of bodily functions. What began as a normal morning quickly turned into a fight for survival. I lost touch with reality as my body shut down, and I was placed on life support, sedated for twenty-four hours, and had a ventilator breathing for me.

During this critical time, the swift actions of those around me were crucial. My eleven-year-old son, Leo, quickly called 911 and took my daughter, Tali, age four, to another room, where they prayed together for their struggling dad. My wife, Kristin, remained by my side, caring for me in every way she could.

I am now on seizure medication, and while I do not anticipate a recurrence, I am making necessary health adjustments to prevent future episodes. All my test results returned normal, and the doctors have been unable to identify a specific cause for the seizures. In a recent EEG report, the doctor shared that my brain was "unremarkable." While that might be tough to hear for most professors, given my circumstances, it was encouraging news. Humor aside, I recognize my recovery as a mystery and grace from God.

To support my health, I have made changes to my daily routine, including reducing stress, improving sleep, and altering my diet—yes, even giving up coffee! For six months, I relied on my family for commutes to work because I was not allowed to drive. I am now equipped with an Apple Watch and a seizure app that closely monitors my heart rate, blood oxygen level, body movements, and other activities. It sends alerts to my family and emergency services if any issues arise.

In the art department at Olivet, we are a community that supports one another as we grow in our artistic skills and abilities. But we are more than that; we care for one another individually—mind, body, and spirit. During my recovery, I received many notes of encouragement, prayers, and acts of kindness and grace from students, colleagues, and administrators.

This experience has reinforced my belief in the importance of community, faith, and resilience. No one facing challenges needs to feel alone. Friends, family, and faith can be relied on for support. Technological, medical, and scientific tools are designed to aid personal efforts. Support networks should be embraced because strength is found by persevering through adversity. Those who look closely will likely be surprised by how many people care. There is goodwill among individuals who want to help.

Life will present challenges that may seem insurmountable, but perseverance, in community with God and neighbor, is the key to overcoming them. Those who wisely build their community, rely on its members, seek expert advice, trust in good counsel, make healthy lifestyle choices, pace themselves, celebrate the process over the final product, and have faith will prevail. They will experience the creative process of persistence.

JON SEALS *was born in Texas and raised in the Appalachian hills of Kentucky. He earned a BS from Olivet, an MAR from Yale Divinity School, and an MFA in painting from Savannah College of Art and Design. A member of Olivet's faculty since 2018, he teaches studio art courses and serves as chair of the Department of Art and Digital Media. He also directs gallery exhibitions for the department. Jon and his wife, Kristin, have two children.*

FINISHING THE RACE
Simone Twibell

"Ah! I can't believe I can run again!" These were the words I uttered after a forced fifteen-year hiatus from doing what I'd always enjoyed.

I started running in high school, mostly for pleasure. I ran long races, half-marathons and the like, all for fun. When I came to Olivet from Brazil as an international student, one of the first classes I took was Nutrition and Exercise. The course was taught by none other than the cross-country coach. When the actual exercise portion of the course came and he saw me running somewhat competitively, he asked if I'd consider joining the team.

"What team?" I asked.

"The cross-country team," he said.

I'd never heard of that sport before coming to the United States, so I wondered, *What in the world is cross-country?*

The image I had when he talked about it was people running across the country, and that didn't sound very fun, especially if I had to cross Iowa or Indiana on foot. He insisted I come to see what it was about, so I did. After going out for a run at Perry Farm, I was hooked. And the coach guaranteed that if we ever ran in Indiana, we would get there by bus.

After training and competing with the Olivet team, I qualified to run the marathon at the NAIA national competition my senior year. In preparation for the race of my life, I trained long hours every day. It wasn't uncommon to have to get up early in the morning and go for a run at the crack of dawn. And it wasn't uncommon to have to do my long runs on a windy day. But, sunshine or rain, I did my best.

When the big day finally came, I was ready for the race. The California weather was sunny and warm, and the paths were lined with fans from across the country. I started slowly, of course. After all, we had twenty-six miles to go. By mile fifteen, I found myself in second place. And, boy, I was sure feeling it. For the next five miles, I competed next to another girl who was not going to let me win easily. By mile nineteen, I thought, *I better speed up if I want to win*. But when I sped up a little, so did she.

Suddenly, at mile twenty-one, the unexpected happened. I hit the famous "runner's wall." If you're a runner, you know what I'm talking about. It's not the greatest feeling. It doesn't matter what you tell your body; it won't respond to your commands. At mile twenty-two, runners were starting to pass me, and by mile twenty-three, I could barely move. I had side stitches, my legs were cramping, and I thought about quitting.

But I heard the voice of my coach along the road: "Keep going! Don't give up now—you're almost there!" With the encouragement of my coach's words, I approached mile twenty-four no longer thinking about quitting. No, now I was thinking about *dying*. It seemed much more likely at the time! But with only two miles left, little by little, I pushed myself until I saw the finish line. As soon as I crossed it, I collapsed and passed out. I was so dehydrated that I became delirious. My coach thought I was speaking Spanish, but God knows it was some sort of angelic tongue preparing me for my eternal home.

Well, I didn't win that day. But I finished the race.

Because that race took so much out of me, I began to experience discomfort in my left knee that continued for years. I couldn't run more than a mile without excruciating pain. To say it was frustrating would be an understatement. I visited doctor after doctor and did all the tests imaginable: MRIs, X-rays, bone scans, compartment syndrome testing, and more. I was determined to do whatever it took so I could go back to doing what I loved. But nothing worked. After the fourth orthopedic doctor told me he couldn't figure out what was wrong with my knee, I didn't think it wise to keep spending money on a self-defeating venture, especially since the previous doctor said it might be mental. I knew it wasn't, but every time I tried to run, my knee hurt again.

If doctors didn't think it was reparable, I reasoned, then maybe God would heal it supernaturally. Every time there was an altar call for healing, I went forward to the altar. But no improvement came. I wanted healing, but more than that, I wanted an answer! It took me fifteen years to finally get a diagnosis. It came from a renowned sports medicine doctor in Chicago who specializes in knee-related issues.

"Your problem is structural," he said.

"Well, if the problem is structural, I want to fix the structure," I said.

"It isn't that easy," came his reply, "and after fifteen years of localized pain, well, there's not much I can do."

I looked at him almost defiantly: "Maybe you can't, but I know God will."

He looked at me as if I were crazy.

Later, I went to a physical therapist who had experience working with athletes. When I told her about my diagnosis, she concluded that the pain was connected to my lower back and hip. She then came up with a plan and saw me three times every week for five straight months. Her strategy included strengthening exercises, stretches, massages, and other remedies. You name it, she did it. I had a lot of homework to do.

Then the unexpected happened. I began to run two miles with no pain, then three miles pain-free, then four, five, seven, ten. I couldn't believe I could run again! In my excitement, I began to sign up for all the races I could possibly do. I started cross-training to regain muscle strength, and began to compete in duathlons and triathlons as well. I thought I'd never run again, let alone competitively, but to my surprise I won my first duathlon in Florida in 2021. I finished my first Half Ironman competition in 2022, and I won my first 5K in 2023. Sure, the competition wasn't as strong as I was used to, but I was pretty happy with my effort.

The writer of Hebrews tells us to "run with perseverance the race marked out for us" (12:1), exhorting us to "strengthen your feeble arms and weak knees. 'Make level paths for your feet'" (12:12–13). The prophet Isaiah gives us a similar message: "Strengthen the feeble hands, steady the knees that give way; say to those with fearful hearts, 'Be strong, do not fear; your God will come'" (35:3–4a). Though the contexts in which the writers penned these words were very different, the message relayed was the same: don't ever lose hope. God's power to restore may take years, but God always shows up to save and heal.

Therefore, fight the good fight, run your race, and keep the faith. This is the only way anyone will finish well.

SIMONE MULIERI TWIBELL *was born in Brazil and spent her childhood years in Argentina. She earned a BA from Olivet and a PhD in intercultural studies from Trinity International University. An Olivet faculty member since 2020, she teaches courses in cross-cultural ministry and missions in the School of Theology and Christian Ministry. Simone resides in Bourbonnais, Illinois, with her son and daughter.*

TWINS, TRIPLETS, AND TUTUS
David Van Heemst

"I'm missing the Yankees game for this," I whispered to my brother-in-law as we sat in the Lincoln Cultural Center for the Arts watching the local girls dance studio perform *The Nutcracker* prior to Christmas. Of course, I knew why I was there. Our five-year-old twins, Maggie and Ellie, were toy soldiers in Act II. We were still early in Act I, though. It was going to be a long time until our daughters would be on stage—and then only for two minutes!

How does a baseball-loving, history-exploring, book-reading guy end up going to a ballet dance recital? I became a girl dad—twins and triplets! All girls! I sure never saw that coming back when I was sitting in my freshman college classes. Now, don't misunderstand. I love being a girl dad. In fact, I believe I've been *called* to be a girl dad. And as the girls get older, I find myself being more surprised, confused, and in love with each of them every day.

Like every child, girls need unconditional love, security, and assurance of significance. Girls need to experience, in the deepest part of their being, that they are safe. They need to feel so deeply valued that their significance level is off the charts. Our girls need their dad's love and affirmation. They also need to learn how to distinguish right from wrong, how to respond openly to gentle guidance, how to develop a strong identity rooted in Jesus, how to connect meaningfully to important people in their lives, and how to develop deep moments of faith while on their individual journeys.

Yikes! That adds up to a daunting list for a dad to consider! Perhaps that explains why, after bringing our three-day-old twins home from the hospital, April and I looked at each other in sheer terror and exclaimed, "We're it! We're their people! It's up to us!" Striving to be a good dad is not for the faint of heart.

I've learned there is one key component that weaves its way through each encounter and the cumulative years of striving to be a good dad: perseverance. Any man worthy of the honor of being called "Dad" must embrace perseverance as the axiomatic variable that forms the foundation of fatherhood. By "perseverance," I mean a long-term commitment that includes showing up, cultivating a relationship, and being fully present. It doesn't mean always knowing the right answer, nor does it mean thinking you're always right. In fact, "I'm sorry" is probably the second-most important phrase to being a good dad, right after, "I love you."

Perseverance is critical for parents from day one. Our day one began when I received a phone call in my ONU basement office in the early fall of 2000. April, calling from Herscher Elementary School where she was teaching, said, "David, the doctor just called. I'm pregnant."

Woohoo! A few weeks later, we went for an ultrasound. The tech said to me, "You might want to sit down."

I asked, "Why?"

She said, "There are two heartbeats. They're twins."

"Oh, my," I said, "You're right. I'd better sit down."

We went from no kids to two kids overnight. Our world was turned upside down. Baseball games were out; late-night feedings were in. Going to the gym was out; singing little songs at their toddler music class—*"Instruments away, instruments away! That is all for us today!"*—was in. One night early on, I volunteered to clean the twins' cloth diapers in the toilet. A fragrant candle was lit, and the yellow rubber gloves were secured. April appreciated the help and thought I was offering to take on the responsibility permanently. The gratitude I witnessed in her eyes and heard in her voice served as a checkmate. I had unknowingly signed up for a two-year assignment!

While going from zero to two daughters overnight was crazy enough, expanding from two daughters to *five* bordered on insanity. When our twins turned six, April gave birth to triplets: Annika, Jessica, and Libby. We then had five daughters under the age of seven. What an experience it was, especially for one who has always taken pride in engaging in philosophical, historical, and political questions. My young children regularly asked me unanswerable questions and took up topics about which I was completely ignorant!

For example, one day Maggie and Ellie informed me that they wanted to play dance and wear their tutus. I had no idea what they were talking about; I had never heard a professor or Yankees broadcaster explain a tutu in all my years. Of course, there were other questions I *was* able to handle, like when Maggie asked me about the difference between Play-Doh and Plato. Or, when we went to the Great Wall Restaurant, and I had to explain to my upset daughter why we weren't at the real Great Wall in China.

The challenges and craziness of life with five daughters can be difficult. For example, when Ellie was three and a half, she contracted viral encephalitis, a life-altering illness. Then the girls' little cousin, George, died on his sixteenth day of life. Later, I became severely sick myself, twice. Ellie and Jessica broke bones. There have been heartaches over breakups, drama with friends, speeding tickets, and driving accidents. For a while, I panicked each time the phone rang, wondering what I might hear next. All our girls were homeschooled. They probably got away with some behavioral things that they wouldn't have gotten away with otherwise, perhaps adding to the chaos.

Surprisingly, however, there is another element: the chaos can also be so much fun. With so many people in our household, there always seems to be a party going on and something to bring a smile to our faces. We've enjoyed plays performed in the attic and front yard, the joys of getting a cat, bedtime routines that include made-up stories about Daphne, watching the Yankees in the playoffs, and hearing the triplets boo every time the archrival Boston Red Sox came to bat.

Through all the challenges and craziness, I've come to realize that it's impossible to persevere alone. April and I have depended on so many other people in our community. Auntie Sarah is absolutely a second mom to the girls. Victoria was a consistent babysitter throughout the girls' first year of life. Grandma Cordes has been a constant, loving, present, Christian example since before the girls were even born. The people at Gathering Point Church of the Nazarene have invested so much into all five girls.

Ultimately, perseverance requires faith and a faithful partner. Scripture and prayer have sustained us. April and I prayed over each of our daughters by name before they were even born. We selected Joshua 24:15b (KJV) as our family verse: "As for me and my house, we will serve the Lord."

April has prayed daily for each of our daughters. She has fasted, seeking wisdom for each of them. One time while she was fasting, I remember her saying, "Oh, David, that half-eaten children's granola bar never looked so good."

We rely on Proverbs 22:6 (KJV): "Train up a child in the way he should go: and when he is old, he will not depart from it." We believe in the beauty of a virtuous woman as described in Proverbs 31. The girls have heard multiple times that the only thing more important than loving Jesus is realizing that Jesus loves them. They have also heard repeatedly, "Van Heemsts give gifts of grace."

God has blessed our decision to persevere and be faithful. Over the years, some of those blessings have included young Ellie wanting me to read her a favorite book, *My Dad Is Great*; Jess coming home from almost anywhere and seeking me out just to reconnect; family bike rides out in the country when preteen Maggie would roll down hills screaming, "As you wish!"; and thirteen-year-old Ellie falling asleep on her bed while reading the Bible and then telling me later that same day, "I can feel Jesus. I can really feel him."

When the twins turned thirteen, in our attempt to launch them into their teen years, we told them that they could go on a trip anywhere. Eschewing Hawaii, they chose to go on a mission trip to Costa Rica. When she was in grade school, Libby loved going with me to Starbucks on Sunday morning for "alone time" before church. All these experiences and more have been the fruit of hanging in there and persisting even when times were hard.

I wrote my fifth book, *Splashing in Puddles: How to Be a Father to Your Daughter* in 2012 to encourage dads to persevere by cultivating a relationship with their daughters. Seeing children grow into adults is phenomenal! Maggie is now a social worker advocating for policy change in Michigan, while Ellie is a sixth-grade science and math teacher in Illinois. The triplets are embarking on the adventure of college as they continue to follow Jesus out into his world. Recently, the triplets and I were coming home from a day at Lake Michigan, laughing and screaming Megan Moroney songs as we traveled. It was the best!

Am I glad that I persevered through dance recitals, dirty diapers, and days of drama? Was it worth enduring broken bones, broken cars, and broken hearts? Is it all right that I missed a few Yankees games and got introduced to tutus? Absolutely! My life has known boundless joy, the result of five daughters and persistence.

DAVID VAN HEEMST *was born and raised in New Jersey. He earned a BA from Dordt College and a PhD in political science from the University of Virginia. He joined the Olivet faculty in 1993, serving as professor of political science and then becoming chair of the Department of History and Political Science. David and his wife, April, are the parents of twin and triplet daughters.*

THE BEST GIFT I NEVER WANTED
Lisa Vander Veer

His hands captivated me the most. How could something so tiny be so intricate? A miniature human hand, with translucent nails and dimples at the base of each finger, wrapping around my finger. I used to stare at those perfect hands for hours as I cradled him close to my heart. It's hard to believe that just nine months earlier, I didn't even want him.

This story begins on the day I successfully defended my doctoral dissertation. You would think a story about persistence would end with finishing a dissertation. Grad school wasn't easy, but I knew how to be a student. Learning how to be a psychologist would come with time. I was giddy with career aspirations as I drove away from school for the last time. I rewarded myself like any good Italian would do—with food. But this time, my celebratory dinner didn't sit well. Part of me already knew, but when the pregnancy test came back positive, I sobbed.

"Mom, something terrible has happened to me." It was nearly midnight, and that was how I greeted my mom when she answered the phone. I sounded more like a fifteen-year-old than a twenty-seven-year-old who had been married for four years. It struck me that, deep down, my plan had been to put off kids until it was too late to have them. I went for a run the following day; it was ninety-five degrees, and I sprinted as if I could escape fate. Suddenly, the image of a poppy seed stopped me in my tracks. The baby was the size of a poppy seed. I was overcome with love for that helpless poppy seed. It was like a switch flipped in that moment and turned on all my maternal instincts.

Paxton was born February 25, 2010. We both had fevers, and my face was mottled with broken blood vessels, his bruised by forceps. After our rough start, Paxton was an easy and healthy baby. He topped the growth charts and hit first-year milestones with ease. He grew to be a pleasant toddler who loved playing with trains and interacting with strangers at the grocery store.

My mom was the first person to notice he didn't babble. It was easy to miss. He told us everything with squeaks and animated gestures. An early intervention therapist started coming to our home to show Paxton flashcards of ordinary objects as a way to awaken speech. He glared at her from his high chair and never said a thing.

My concern grew in the year leading up to Paxton's eventual diagnosis of childhood apraxia of speech (CAS), which is a rare speech disorder where the brain cannot properly direct the jaw, mouth, and tongue to speak even when the desire, intellect, and physical ability are present. We were celebrating his third birthday at Mayo Clinic, seeking reasons for his silence. That diagnosis launched intensive speech, developmental, physical, vision, social, and occupational therapy.

"Progress determines prognosis," his therapists would say.

Over the next eleven years, Paxton would receive many other labels: motor apraxia, dyspraxia, developmental coordination disorder, dysgraphia, dyslexia, pragmatic communication disorder, attention deficit disorder, panic disorder, social anxiety, major depressive disorder with suicidal thoughts, and, most recently, autism spectrum disorder. Diagnoses give a frame but no picture.

Really, this is Paxton's story, and maybe one day he will tell it. But this story is also mine because I have watched every uphill battle and have wondered why Paxton *and* God were both so silent. Shortly after his first visit to Mayo Clinic, an angel disguised as a speech therapist figured out that Paxton didn't know how to coordinate breathing with intentional sound production. She laid him on the floor and pushed on his stomach to help him connect exhaling with sounds. In a few months, he was uttering several fragmented words. I hoped those few words would blow open a levee and speech would pour out. Instead, words came like rusty drips from a faucet. I gradually relinquished hope that this would progress to conversational skills.

Paxton had to do everything a thousand times in order to learn it. While other kids were moving on to play dates and playground games, we were practicing two-syllable words and putting on a shirt without becoming a tangle of arms and elbows. Paxton swallowed questionable amounts of toothpaste before grasping how to spit it out in sixth grade. Constructs like imagination, self-advocacy, and understanding sarcasm took years. Junior high brought a rapid acceleration of interpersonal concepts like conflict, romance, and social media—he would prefer to avoid them. There are so many building blocks in a human life that we take for granted. They manifested mysteriously for Paxton's athletic younger brothers and spirited baby sister.

Paxton has normal intelligence, with relative math and verbal comprehension strengths, but his apraxia betrays him. Apraxia, whether speech or motor, is like having action steps printed on scattered puzzle pieces. Before action can be initiated, those puzzle pieces must be sorted and assembled in the correct order. For most people, the motor-planning systems operate behind the scenes.

"How old are you?" his pediatrician asked him during his pre-high school physical.

Paxton looked panicked and blurted out that he didn't know.

"Fourteen," I prompted. "You're fourteen." Paxton knows that. Paxton knows many things, but he also knows that by the time he regulates his anxiety enough to retrieve the information and then organizes the motor action to say it, his pediatrician will already think he is an idiot. The world won't wait for Paxton to put together his puzzle pieces.

Woody Webb was Olivet's vice president of student development, and my boss, during most of Paxton's childhood. In one of our first meetings, Woody opened with a passage from Isaiah that changed me forever: "When you pass through the waters, I will be with you; and when you pass through the rivers, they will not sweep over you. When you walk through the fire, you will not be burned; the flames will not set you ablaze. For I am the LORD your God, the Holy One of Israel, your Savior" (Isaiah 43:2–3a). Woody reminded us that being Christian doesn't keep us from trouble, but the Lord promises to be with us through the trouble.

The Lord's faithfulness is abundantly clear. He blessed Paxton with heroic teachers and therapists who performed small miracles. Paxton is determined and principled—the embodiment of Romans 5:3–5. Tall and oblivious to his handsome features, he describes himself as "a back-of-the-room kind of guy." He has been the best friend anyone could ask for to the few who were patient enough to get to know him. He recently started high school with a thousand kids in his freshman class, but he sits alone at lunch. I wish I could morph into a teenager and introduce myself while sliding my cafeteria tray next to his. Faith is living with open hands.

Paxton used to ask me how my day was, and no matter my response, he would shrug and reply, "That's all I've got." He has come a long way. We have conversations now, and his dry humor is amusing. I can tell he is still piecing together the concept of conversation, but lately he has responded to irony with a smirk of recognition. Some days, I forget about the dark clouds that brought us to this point or the uncharted territory that lies ahead.

Being a parent is the gift I never wanted, but it's the best gift I've ever received. It's the best gift, even though the little hands I used to hold are now large and clumsy. I would die for Paxton, not because of his potential to do great things in the world—although he will—but because I love who he is, just as he is. I get glimpses of how the Lord sees us: created in his image and treasured, even in our diminished state. When I worry about the future, I remember that God loves Paxton, and all of us, more than we've ever loved anything. Our finite brains can't comprehend that kind of love. We can persist with peace, knowing the Lord's plans are immeasurably greater than our own.

LISA VANDER VEER was born and raised in the south suburbs of Chicago. She earned a BA from Wheaton College and an MA in counseling and PsyD from the Adler School of Professional Psychology. She joined Olivet in 2009 as a therapist and director of the Counseling and Health Services Office. She currently serves as dean of student persistence. Lisa and her husband, Steve, have four children.

31
SISTER MARY ROSE
Aggie Veld

I grew up in Fort Myers, Florida, where I attended Bishop Verot Catholic High School. In fact, as the tenth of eleven children, I was one of two family members to attend a private Catholic school throughout the twelve years of elementary and secondary education. I was born curious, and that characteristic made me a good student, evidenced by the fact that I routinely earned good grades throughout those formative years.

Of course, living in a home with so many children meant that in our early years we sometimes had to go without things we wanted. For example, I never had a backpack for my books. Instead, I stuffed my papers and books into my dad's old briefcase and carried it back and forth to school. Compared to the standards of my peers, I was odd and often felt like an outsider. Yet my parents were loving, and growing up was a joyful and busy time that laid a firm foundation of faith, resourcefulness, and a love for learning.

I was very serious and spent a lot of time thinking about meaningful things in life. I was particularly fascinated with the environment and connections between biology and everyday life. The companionship I enjoyed with my ten siblings provided solace, whereas the world of nature around me invited me to explore its intricacies.

As I grew older, my dad made a few financial investments that did well, making it possible for me to go to college—a luxury not afforded to many of my older siblings. I was one of just three children in my family to attend college. However, my dad's financial turn was only one factor that led to my current work as a university professor. The other significant factor was the influence of Sister Mary Rose.

I wandered through my school years knowing that I liked science—biology in particular. Beyond that, I was aimless in my academic pursuits. Sister Mary Rose, my high school principal, must have noticed that because one day she called me to her office. She had the wisdom to advise me how to study and prepare for the academic rigors that lay ahead of me. She wanted to help me take my academic efforts to a new level. She knew I was likely headed to college, where the expectations would be very different from anything I had yet known.

Sister Mary Rose took the initiative to show me a simple study strategy that changed my world forever. Identifying my interest in science, she encouraged me to take my science textbook, read the appropriate chapter the night before the classroom lecture, and then take notes during the lecture. She encouraged me to rewrite those same notes within twenty-four hours. This was to be done on three-holed, college-ruled, looseleaf paper with an extended left margin, using a standard formal outline format with main points and sub-points and sub-sub-points.

She continued by showing me how to write the notes on the right two-thirds of the page, thereby leaving the left side for later additions, short explanations, and acronyms I made up for repeated phrases. Further, I was to write only on one side of the paper, number the pages, three-hole-punch any handouts, arrange them in the lecture sequence, and keep all my notes in a three-ring binder. To continue the process, she encouraged me to rewrite the notes on scrap paper from memory. I should go as far as I could without checking the completed outline, then look beyond where I was able to recall and start again from the beginning until I could recreate the entire outline without checking. The process—repetition and creation of the notes in my own handwriting—helped solidify the material in my memory. I was amazed at the difference this made. The night before an exam, all I had to do was read through the notes one more time. Most of the work had already been done.

Using this method, I learned. I mean, I really learned! Concepts and ideas in lectures started making sense. I could connect the dots that at one time seemed so random. I finally had a way to bridge the analytic world of academia to my way of learning. I found a strategy that worked for me; I found my pace! My new mantra became, "I am capable at a pace."

This strategy from Sister Mary Rose not only helped me as I finished high school but also proved invaluable as I earned both bachelor's and master's degrees in science education at the University of Florida. For years, I relied on the advice she had offered me long ago in her office. My sense of debt to her grew. How could I have ever succeeded without her practical advice? How did she know what I would need to persist in my academic journey?

Nearly two decades later, the ultimate test came when I was in the middle of my doctoral program. I never would have made it without Sister Mary Rose's earlier guidance and instruction, her encouragement to develop an academic work ethic, and her passion for helping others succeed in finding their calling. Her insistence that I give this learning strategy a try made a difference for which I will always be thankful.

Some fifteen years ago, I was able to call Sister Mary Rose from my office at Olivet. What a delightful exchange we had. I reminded her of our office visit and of her coaching and encouragement back at Bishop Verot. Then I told her about my academic journey since leaving Fort Myers. I informed her of my current faculty position in the Department of Biology at Olivet and thanked her for helping me write the rest of my story.

She has since passed away, but I think of her often as I watch part of her live on in new generations of students. I now teach this same strategy to my students who are looking for a new way to approach their studies. In fact, I keep pads of scrap paper, packages of three-holed, college-ruled, looseleaf paper, three-ring binders, rulers, and three-hole punches in my office for those who are willing to try the study skill. Like Sister Mary Rose did for me, I walk any student who expresses interest through the same process that was once shared with me.

Over the years, I have come to call this method the SMR Study Skills Strategy. SMR, I tell my students, stands for "simply more repetition." Of course, in my heart I know it also stands for "Sister Mary Rose," without whom I would not have persevered through the rigors of education to where I am today.

AGGIE VELD *was born and raised in Florida. She earned a BS in science education from the University of Florida and a PhD in professional studies in education from Capella University. A member of Olivet's faculty since 2005, she teaches courses in biology and science education. Aggie has four children and eleven grandchildren and lives with her husband, Paul, in Bourbonnais, Illinois.*

32
LOVE WINS
Laura Widstrom

I first learned about foster care when I was around middle school age. Once my mind wrapped around the concept, I knew it would be part of my life calling. No matter where God led me in life—geographically, vocationally, or in marital status—I sensed that being a foster mom was to be part of the package. My motivation was rooted in my Christian values and intrinsically from my own upbringing. After my dad died when I was four and my mom grew distant, I felt like I was raising myself. It was a lonely endeavor, and I didn't want that for any other kid. If I could, I wanted to be the constant and the advocate for a child who needed one.

After serving on staff at a church for more than a decade and finishing grad school, I began the second chapter of my adult life as a university professor, providing me with a more predictable schedule. Then I signed up to train for and receive my foster-parenting license. Within hours after my availability was posted, my first call came.

Foster care is an adventure like no other. The training mandated by the state barely touches the surface. Sometimes, with just an hour's notice, your life can be turned upside down as a child is brought to your doorstep, often with only the clothes on their back. The information accompanying the child is always incomplete, and as time passes and the full picture emerges, you find yourself knee-deep in unfamiliar waters. Thankfully, foster parents tend to network and find one another, grateful for the support of others who understand. Through my experiences, I have met some of the most Christlike families, whose testimony and tenacity have guided and encouraged me forward.

My foster-care license was open for seven years, and seven children came through my home. The shortest stay was only a month because Child Protective Services determined the nine-year-old in my care was not living in her home state; paperwork followed to get her back home. That girl did not know how bedsheets worked because she had never slept in a bed. I then had two brothers for a year whose birth parents battled addiction. The court gave the parents one more try, and they returned home. A few years later, the boys were back in care, then back with their dad as the cycle continued. I had a little boy who bounced in and out of my home three times before he stayed. At one point, two of his brothers were also with me. One brother stayed, and the other moved on. I eventually adopted those two remaining brothers as my sons. After the placement of five boys in a row, I begged my agency not to call me for a boy again. My heart needed a girl, though I knew I could never say no to any child who needed a safe home.

I waited about a year. My boys and I had just gotten back from a summer trip two weeks before the fall semester started. We were exhausted, the fridge was empty, and the laundry pile was noteworthy. I received a call asking if we would take a newborn girl who was healthy aside from drug exposure, which had unknown long-term implications. I said of course. We did not know how long our girl would stay. Visits were scheduled with her birth parents, but they never came. After a series of complex court appearances, the judge decided neither of the birth parents was able to provide adequate care, so just after her second birthday, I was able to adopt the girl.

Adoption comes with many unknowns. I have no contact with the birth families of my three children, so I do not know their full medical histories. While each experienced trauma, there is no way to predict how the trauma will impact them or at what stage of life the impact will be most profound. As my children grow, we encounter new challenges I never anticipated when I welcomed chubby toddlers into my home and scooped up a newborn from the NICU. This raises the nature-versus-nurture question. How much can a stable home with a loving parent and the support of a village overcome the impact of physical abuse, neglect, substance abuse, and domestic violence? Researchers affirm that, while the brains of young children may have no conscious memories, their bodies remember. This truth persists especially for my daughter, whose trauma experience was primarily in utero.

My children's daily needs are significant and hold space on our family calendar. They each require care from several specialists along with additional support at school. My family requires a routine that is different from a traditional family. Routine and consistency are very important, making travel difficult. All the children need their own bedroom for sleeping and breaks to regulate, so sharing a hotel room is not ideal. Every night at dinner, we talk through the plan for the following day alongside a large calendar that helps everyone visualize what comes next. Consistent sleep, mealtime schedules, and careful monitoring of nutrition are important. Festivals and events with loud music and crowds are overwhelming, so we do our best to focus on low-key outdoor activities.

Each of my children needs a lot of support to handle the highs and lows of daily life. Each has the potential to lash out aggressively, which is difficult for outsiders to navigate. Therefore, babysitters come minimally. In the past seven years, I have been away for one weekend conference, and the friend who watched my children said, "No more." We engage in less technology than most families and lean toward athletics in an attempt to channel energy positively. My children each participate in sports year round to practice a healthy outlet and develop coping skills. Olivet's indoor recreational center is a wonderful gift on winter days.

I will be quick to admit that I am simultaneously building *and* flying the plane as I parent three children with unique needs. There is no manual aside from Scripture, which is full of stories of Jesus loving and engaging others even when doing so was messy and complicated. At the end of God's story, love wins. Though I do not know what that will look like for my family as the hormones settle and adults emerge, I persist in my investment in these three lives that have been entrusted to me, and I do it because Jesus persisted.

In the end, I anticipate that love will win.

LAURA WIDSTROM *was born and raised in Rockford, Illinois, where she also served a local church for thirteen years. She earned her BA from Trinity Christian College and her PhD from Trinity International University. Laura joined the Olivet faculty in 2021 and serves as an associate professor of youth ministry in the School of Theology and Christian Ministry. She is a mom to three children, and together they enjoy playing soccer and boating at their family cottage in Michigan.*

NO BACKGROUND FOR SUCCESS
Neal Woodruff

My dad was born into a Depression-era farming family in rural Kansas. Money and food were scarce, and the work was hard. Like many farm kids, Dad often missed school to work on the farm. His parents had only a few years of education between them. Believing he and his brothers would get "uppity" if they had too much schooling, they pulled all three boys out of school entirely just as Dad was ready to start high school. Still, Dad had a passion for education.

Dad used the education he did have as a supply sergeant during the Korean conflict. During his off-duty time, he would regularly run several miles to a Korean village to teach English to the villagers before running back to the base. Little did anyone know at the time that this was the beginning of what would become a lifelong teaching career.

Upon returning home from his duties in Korea, he attempted to enroll in a college close to home through the GI Bill. When he met with the registrar, Dad was told he didn't have the necessary background to be successful in college studies. Dad, however, was determined to get an education.

The registrar eventually told him he might be allowed to enroll for a degree if he could first successfully complete a year of college basics for no credit. Dad jumped in and began doing the necessary work. After successfully completing that year and his college degree some years later, my dad, William Woodruff, went on to teach public school, pastor churches, learn nine languages, edit portions of the Old Testament for the New International Version of the Bible, and eventually serve as professor of biblical studies and biblical languages at Olivet from 1968 to 1992.

I didn't have the obstacles to education that Dad experienced. Both Dad and Mom were lifelong educators, so it was simply expected that I would get an education, and they sacrificed many things to help make it a reality. Still, history has an odd way of repeating itself. When I sought entrance to doctoral studies at a highly regarded music program, I met with a well-known musical scholar teaching there at the time. He perused my transcripts, including one from Olivet, and concluded that I didn't have the necessary background to be successful in rigorous graduate studies. Specifically, in his experience, Christians weren't interested in serious music scholarship and were most often satisfied with musical mediocrity. He eventually told me I might be allowed to enroll as a non-degree student for one semester. I took him up on the offer. When that semester was over, I enrolled again, and kept enrolling, assuming he would let me know when I failed to measure up to his standard.

A few semesters later, I was assigned to present a musical analysis of Benjamin Britten's *Cantata misericordium* in front of the graduate students in the program. The text is taken from the parable of the good Samaritan, but this cantata was not originally intended for use in church services. The music is dense and complex, and as I posed questions during the presentation, the most obvious answers came from the biblical story itself. Just like in movies or TV shows, the music was used to convey ideas, thoughts, and emotions that went beyond the plain dialogue—things like excitement, sorrow, or suspense. The musical themes I was discussing were used in similar ways based on the narrator's expectation of compassion as the Levite and priest approached, contrasted with despair and disbelief when they passed by. The same musical motives were then changed in subtle but significant ways when expressing disdain as the Samaritan approached, along with surprise and a musically transformed sense of disbelief when the Samaritan paused to care for the traveler.

Without an understanding of the scriptural context, many of these changes went unnoticed or appeared trivial or anomalous to some of the other students. As it turned out, my Christian background was integral to a scholarly presentation of the music. After this presentation, my professor pulled me aside to say it was time for me to formally apply to the program. This same professor, who was initially uncertain about my ability to succeed in serious graduate studies, even recommended that some doctoral students who followed later in the program ask me for recommendations on how to prepare for the general exams. After performing, teaching in public schools and other universities, and ministering as a pastoral musician, I accepted the call to teach at Olivet in 2000.

I wonder what would have happened if Dad hadn't persisted past the educational challenges of his childhood—if he had surrendered to the family and financial difficulties or taken at face value the assumption that he wasn't good enough for college. Although I didn't understand it at the time, I experienced evidence of his work when I was a child and he invited students from his Greek and Hebrew classes to have breakfast in our home. Everyone had to translate a verse of Scripture before eating, and I watched him patiently help them work through the process. I'm reminded of his perseverance often, such as when his former students tell of his grace working with them to overcome their own personal and educational obstacles—a grace born out of his own experience and struggle.

I wonder how my own life and career path would be different if I had listened to someone tell me I didn't have the background to be successful in graduate studies. I get to see the fruits of this endurance every day. I see it when students take seriously the call to discipline themselves to do the hard work of becoming skilled musicians, and when they own that musical mediocrity is poor stewardship of God's gifts, realizing that "holy shoddy is still shoddy." I see it in the lives of former students who demonstrate musical excellence as educators, performers, music therapists, and pastoral musicians seeking to steward their musical skills to make a kingdom difference in the world.

Dad, who supposedly didn't have the necessary background to be successful and had to take a year of college courses for no credit, went on to earn more than eight hundred hours of mostly graduate-level college credit. In his retirement, he fulfilled a lifelong ambition by earning his doctorate. In fact, Dad and I completed our doctorates within just a few weeks of each other in 2002. I can't help but wonder where evidence of this endurance and determination will show up next.

NEAL WOODRUFF *was born and raised in Bourbonnais, Illinois. He earned a BA in music education from Olivet and a DMA from the University of Oklahoma. A member of Olivet's faculty since 2000, he has taught music courses, performed vocally, and conducted several ensembles over the years. He currently serves as the associate dean of the School of Music. Neal and his wife, Shannon, have one son and two daughters.*

THE OLIVET STORY
John Bowling

Editor's Note: The preceding chapters have been personal stories from Olivet Nazarene University faculty members focusing on how persistence helped them navigate a challenge or season of life. This final chapter is a story by President Emeritus John C. Bowling, who reveals that persistence has also been central to the history, development, and preservation of Olivet as an educational institution. In simple terms, were it not for the determination and perseverance of Olivet's leaders across the years, there would be no university today. Persistence is part of our institutional DNA.

Olivet Nazarene University began in the minds and hearts of a handful of eastern Illinois families during the first decade of the twentieth century. Remarkable events were taking place at the time that would alter how people lived. The world was changing in fundamental ways that had never happened in the long history of humanity. Electricity, for example, made the night seem like day. It revolutionized industry and illuminated homes and cities. The invention of the automobile not only made travel easier but also signaled a wholesale change in American society. Soon, there was even talk of people flying! The world was changing.

Those changes, however, extended beyond technology and industry to the way people thought. In 1905 Albert

Einstein published his first general theory of relativity, which began to turn our understanding of the physical world upside down. About the same time, in Vienna, a psychiatrist named Sigmund Freud began to write and talk about human personality in ways that were new. His views of human sexuality sent a kind of shiver around the world. Just a few decades earlier, the British scientist Charles Darwin had published his 1859 book *The Origin of Species*, challenging how humans understood the beginning of life itself. All these new ideas—Darwin's theories, Freud's analysis, Einstein's contributions, along with many others—combined to reshape how people viewed the world.

During that same period, a small group of devoted men and women recognized that the world their children were about to inherit would be a much different world than the one they had known. This realization prompted the idea of establishing a first-rate college where their children and others could prepare for a world that had not yet arrived. With a great measure of faith and sacrifice, they began to examine what it would take to launch a college, and they soon started to raise money and dream. Then, in the fall of 1907, in the little town called Georgetown, Illinois, about ninety miles south of the present campus, what we know today as Olivet Nazarene University was born. There was one teacher named Mary Nesbitt, one classroom, and a handful of students.

During that first year, in 1907–1908, the founders of the school pooled their resources. They mortgaged farms, sold property, and dipped into their savings to purchase two large farms that were adjacent to each other, just south of Georgetown. Once the property had been secured, they began to lay out an elaborate plan. At the heart of the property, with frontage on Illinois Route 1 and alongside the Illinois railroad, they envisioned building a college campus. A new town eventually took shape around their dream. It was called Olivet. Soon, construction began on the farmland and, before long, the school moved from Georgetown to the new property at Olivet. As brick buildings were completed, students started coming from areas throughout Illinois, from neighboring Indiana, and from as far away as Ohio.

Within five years, nearly two hundred students had enrolled. The founding families eventually became overwhelmed with the responsibility of caring for the school and its students while still running their farms and businesses. Realizing they could not continue the initiative with their limited resources, yet not wanting to give up on their educational dream, they offered their young school in 1912 to a brand-new Christian denomination. The Church of the Nazarene agreed to take control of the college at Olivet. You might say it was a match made in heaven. The young denomination suddenly had a college, and the college had an expanded constituency. The school continued to grow and mature over the coming years; new buildings were added to accommodate the needs.

During those early years, as one might expect, there was immense financial pressure on the school. Everything was new and had to be purchased or built from scratch. Modest tuition was charged, but mounting expenses demanded the support of friends and families of the college. These efforts failed to relieve the increasing financial burden. Therefore, in 1926, Olivet reached a point where it had no choice but to declare bankruptcy. It appeared the eastern Illinois farmers' dream had reached its end. Bankruptcy meant that the court stepped in and moved to sell the assets of the college; creditors had to be paid. Despite its strong and promising start, the school faced closure.

Word spread that the college's assets would be sold. The date was set for a public auction in Danville, Illinois. A large crowd gathered because many hoped to buy the land or pieces of equipment at a steep discount. When the appointed time came and the bidding process began, something remarkable happened.

A tall, relatively young man with a strong voice standing at the back of the crowd spoke up and offered to buy everything. This declaration startled the rest of the crowd, who had all come prepared to bid on an item or two; no one else there was prepared to buy *everything*. That single bid could not be matched, the auction abruptly ended, and all the assets of the school were sold to one man, Dr. T. W. Willingham.

Dr. Willingham had been a member of the board of trustees at the college and was distraught at the bankruptcy. He immediately began a one-man crusade to save the school. He went to congregations and businesses, and to nearly everyone he knew, saying, "We've got to save Olivet." People took second mortgages. They gave sacrificially until there was finally enough money to buy the school. Dr. Willingham was elected president of Olivet the day after the auction and continued in that role for thirteen years. Under his capable leadership, the school continued to gain support and grow, surviving even when the dark clouds of the Great Depression settled across the nation.

Though things were still tight, the future of the college seemed promising. Then, unexpectedly, tragedy struck late on a Saturday night in October 1939. A massive fire broke out on the campus. Being a very small town, Olivet did not have a fire department, so village folks along with faculty, staff, and students carried water themselves in hopes of containing the flames. Word was sent to nearby Danville for help, but by the time the Danville Fire Department got to the school, it was too late. As the sun rose the next Sunday morning, much of the campus lay before them in ashes. In shock, faculty, staff, and students stood in a limp circle and looked on helplessly as their hopes, dreams, and sacrifices smoldered before their eyes.

Students reported watching the fire as it spread. One individual spoke of hearing pianos dropping through the floors as the buildings burned. It was a dramatic moment. How could the school ever come back from such a devastating loss? Furthermore, the effects of the Great Depression were still being felt, and war clouds gathered over Europe. What chance did Olivet have to recover from its ashes at such a bleak time?

Then, just two days later, another remarkable event happened. It did not happen on the campus. It did not even happen in Illinois. It occurred a thousand miles away from Olivet in Boston, Massachusetts. On that morning, just after the fire, a businessman perused the morning edition of *The Boston Globe*. His eyes fell on a story—really, it was little more than a headline with a couple of sentences—that read, "Olivet College, Olivet, Illinois, Destroyed by Fire." The businessman made a mental note and went on about his day.

Later that morning while he was at his office, the headline came back to him. He got up from his desk and walked down the hall to a large filing room. There, he found the file drawer marked "I" and worked his way back through the files until he came to "Illinois." From the drawer, he pulled out a folder marked "Olivet College, Olivet, Illinois." The Boston insurance company where he worked had a policy on the campus in Olivet, Illinois. Although the insurance money would not be enough to rebuild the campus, there were some funds available that might help the school through its crisis.

Perhaps the most amazing part of the story is that, as the man in Massachusetts was going through the Illinois file looking for Olivet College, he came across another folder marked "St. Viator's College, Bourbonnais, Illinois." St. Viator's College, once a fine school, had been started in Bourbonnais in the mid-1800s by the Roman Catholic Church. It prospered for many years before closing its doors during the Great Depression as the Catholic Church consolidated some of its schools. A thousand miles away, two days after the fire at Olivet, with the scent of smoke still in the air, a man stood in his office in Boston pondering the situation. In one hand he had an Illinois college without a campus, and in the other hand he had an Illinois campus without a college.

The insurance company made a proposal to settle the insurance claim on the Olivet property by offering the college the campus in Bourbonnais at a much-reduced rate. After an Olivet delegation made the trip to Bourbonnais to look over the campus, they decided to accept the offer. The school limped along and finished its year at the Olivet location. Then, in the summer of 1940, what was left in terms of equipment and supplies was transported to Bourbonnais.

Four buildings—now known as Chapman Hall, Burke Administration, Miller Business Center, and Birchard Gymnasium—stood on forty acres of land that were once home to St. Viator's College. Olivet's arrival in Bourbonnais in 1940 marked the beginning of a new day. The school moved from the cornfields of central Illinois to a fully developed campus within striking distance of Chicago. An overwhelmed church leader who visited the campus at the time said, "I don't know how you'll ever fill this place up! It seems so grand."

The school quickly began to regroup and find its footing once again. Throughout the next several decades, Olivet paid off the remaining debt on the new campus and experienced steady growth and expansion.

The college has stood the test of time; its leaders never gave up on the dream of those early farmers. Now recognized as a university, the school endured some tough years that included bankruptcy, the Great Depression, and a destructive fire. Those experiences were precursors to other crises in the form of wars, recessions, tornadoes, untimely deaths of students and staff, a pandemic, and more. Through all those turbulent times, Olivet not only survived but thrived as a university. The initial 40 acres and 4 buildings have now multiplied to a campus of 270 acres and more than 30 buildings.

How did that happen amid such adversity? Two factors stand out. First, the unwavering persistence of visionary leaders kept the school moving forward when financial ruin and campus calamity threatened its undoing. Simply stated, Olivet Nazarene University exists because its forefathers and foremothers refused to give up. Second, the university has maintained a clear and distinct mission: to provide an *education with a Christian purpose*. Commitment to that mission has motivated generations of faculty, staff, and students to pursue excellence and make a positive difference even during uncertain times.

The twin pillars of persistence and mission have repeatedly sustained the university when fierce winds—so common across the flat farmlands of Illinois—have threatened its ruin. The university still rests on those same pillars today.

JOHN BOWLING *was born and raised in Ohio. He earned his BA from Olivet and holds two doctorate degrees: an EdD from Southwestern Seminary and a DMin from Southern Methodist University. He has served the Church of the Nazarene as a pastor, teacher, author, and university president. He has the distinction of being Olivet's longest-tenured president, having held that role from 1991 until 2021. He and his wife, Jill, currently divide their time between Michigan and Illinois.*

PRAYER FOR PERSISTENCE

O Sovereign Lord, who watches over and sustains the entire world,
    Thank you for never abandoning me.
Though I have too often demanded my stubborn way and struggled to remain faithful,
    You have never given up on me.
Though I have dishonored you at times by not treating others as I should,
    You have never given up on me.
Though my words have sometimes been hurtful and my pride has gotten the best of me,
    You have never given up on me.

O Lord Jesus, who endured the cross with its pain and shame on behalf of a needy world,
    Thank you for standing by me.
Though I have too often been ashamed to speak a word of witness on your behalf,
    You have never given up on me.
Though I have not always walked and talked like you while claiming to be a Christian,
    You have never given up on me.
Though I have been far too hesitant to pick up my own cross daily and follow you,
    You have never given up on me.

Prayer for Persistence

As I navigate this fallen and broken world with its multiple challenges,
    Thank you for your presence and strength that encourage me.
Though adversity, unfairness, and difficulty at times sweep over me like a tidal wave,
    Help me never to give up on you.
Though burdens mount, the workload increases, and anxiety rises around me,
    Help me never to give up on you.
Though loss, pain, and stress come unexpectedly and threaten to overwhelm me,
    Help me never to give up on you.

May any suffering that I experience produce perseverance,
    And may that perseverance produce character[*]
    So that, in every circumstance, others will see you through me
    As I press toward the goal and receive the prize that Christ Jesus has for me.[**]

Amen.

---

[*] Romans 5:3–4
[**] Philippians 3:14

www.ingramcontent.com/pod-product-compliance
Lightning Source LLC
Chambersburg PA
CBHW070148100426
42743CB00013B/2853